Scrappy

Scrappy

Use Everything You Have, Trust Yourself,
and Press the Reset Button for Success,
the Lolly Wolly Doodle Way

BRANDI TEMPLE

St. Martin's Press 🅼 New York

www.stmartins.com

Designed by Steven Seighman

The Library of Congress Cataloging-in-Publication Data is available upon request.

ISBN 978-1-250-08809-3 (hardcover)
ISBN 978-1-250-08810-9 (e-book)

Our books may be purchased in bulk for promotional, educational, or business use. Please contact your local bookseller or the Macmillan Corporate and Premium Sales Department at 1-800-221-7945, extension 5442, or by e-mail at MacmillanSpecialMarkets@macmillan.com.

First Edition: May 2017

10 9 8 7 6 5 4 3 2 1

To Shana Fisher for believing in me, for always telling me the truth no matter how great or how hurtful it might be, and for teaching me that you can only get two seats at a board meeting, and in life: one in which you can say, "F*@# you," or one where somebody is saying that to you.

And to the late Frank Laney, who showed me what true love, humility, and friendship look like. He will live forever in my heart.

Author's Note

This is a true story. However, a few names and details have been changed.

Contents

Acknowledgments

To my Heavenly Father... Thank You for Your grace, mercy, and forgiveness, for without that, I would be nothing. Thank You for blessing me with this incredible story and enabling me to tell the good, the bad, and the ugly. To You I give all the praise.

To Clay, thanks for allowing me to be part of your life. You taught me that a mother's love doesn't have to start at birth.

To Kade, thanks for being my "first love" and helping me to realize that love is bigger than the biggest mud puddle in the world. It is endless.

To Vivi, thank you for sharing me (even when you didn't want to), for the morning rides that made my day, and for a love that is just as beautiful as you are and weighs three pounds.

To Bella, thank you for your amazing heart that is so full of compassion and understanding, and for sharing the best snuggles in the world with me. Thanks for loving me to Pluto and back.

To Will, thanks for being "my person." For being there when I get home at night, for making sure I never run out of DDP, and for making sure it's never boring. Love you more.

To my mom and dad, I'm filled with gratitude for your endless encouragement, for believing in me when I didn't, and most of all for allowing me to fail and "figure it out for myself" so that I could become the woman I am today. Three pounds!

To Mammaw, even though I can't tell you how much you are a part of my story face-to-face, I know you can see it. Thank you for being my style curator, my sewing teacher, my shopping guide, and my biggest fan.

To Donnie and Patrick for never taking it easy on me, for teaching me to be tough, strong, and independent. Thanks for allowing me to take the "wall space" and for never letting me forget where I came from. The two best brothers in the world. Love you both!

To Ashley Eilbacher, for being the "wind beneath my wings" (sorry, I couldn't resist). You are my "bestest" friend. Thank you for your endless support, your endless wisecracks and eye rolls and, most important, your endless friendship.

To Steve Summers, thank you for taking me under your wing and moving me forward. Your countless stories, your hilarious sayings, and even the endless bantering back and forth are what got me through some of the darkest times. To Rhonda Summers–thanks for your friendship, support, and generosity as you graciously shared Steve's time with me and put up with his endless LWD stories.

To all my Doodle family, who are far too many to single out, thank you for giving me the great honor of being your "Circus Master." It's been a roller-coaster ride. At times, it's felt like I've traveled to hell and back, yet you never wavered in your support of me. You stuck by me through thick and thin and thin and, no matter where this story ends, I know that I have been loved, befriended, and even cursed by the most amazing people on this earth. Thank you for being you, for not compromising, and for allowing me to be *me*.

To Samantha Marshall, thanks for putting up with the worst procrastinating, ADHD, OCD subject you've ever had to deal with. Without you there would only be words and not a beautiful story to share.

To Andy McNicol, thanks for pursuing me and convincing me that I had a story to tell. Your patience and support have been invaluable.

To Nicole Williams, your patience and persistence have kept this whole train moving.

And last but not least, Elizabeth Beier. I cannot thank you enough for your brilliant ideas, gentle guidance, and unbridled enthusiasm. You always believed there was a book in me, and you brought out the best. I couldn't have done it without you.

Introduction

Ah-Ha!

I can, with one eye squinted,
take it all as a blessing.

–FLANNERY O'CONNOR

ight years ago, if you had told me I'd be the CEO of a national women and children's clothing brand that revolution- ized the retail business model through Facebook and end up on the cover of a magazine, I'd have looked at you sideways. Who, me? An entrepreneur? You must be crazy! I had no aspirations to run a business. Heck, I didn't even know what social media was. I was just another stressed-out mom trying to make ends meet.

Like a lot of jobs hit by the recession, my husband's job selling heavy equipment for the construction industry was in jeopardy, so I figured I'd contribute what I could by sewing and selling children's clothes. It wouldn't be much, just a few extra dollars, but at the very least it might earn me some man- icure money. After all, no matter how bad times get, a South- ern girl has to keep up appearances.

Little did I know what was in store for us. A path opened up that I never even realized existed. This isn't the story of a dream come true. This is what happens when life exceeds your wildest imagination. And it can happen to anyone, anytime, with the right mixture of common sense, endurance, doggedness, and faith.

Above all, you have to be open to what God is telling you. Whatever your belief system, there's a higher wisdom at work, and it can come in the form of your inner voice, intuition, a sudden and seemingly random intervention. . . . I call it God, you may choose to call it something else, but either way it's real, and you have to find those moments to tune out the noise, be still, pay attention, and listen. Whether it's a complete sense of peace about a decision you've made or a truth that hits you like a lightning bolt, God has a funny way of letting you know when you are on the right road. I call these subtle signposts my "ah-ha" moments, and they've occurred at every major turning point in my life.

They happen when things come full circle. Think back to those times when something happened that made no sense, and weeks, months, even years later, it all becomes clear. I used to get so stuck in the past, wondering, "Why me? Why did I have to go through that? Why was I there?" Life seemed so random and unfair at times. But as my story unfolded, I realized that everything happens for a reason. Nothing is wasted, and each experience has been stitched together to create a beautiful whole. Life is a big university, and there are lessons to be learned in every situation, good, bad, even silly.

My big brother Donnie used to torture me, using every opportunity he could to bust my beauty-queen bubble. He used to drive me to the movies, where I would meet my friends, the "in" crowd in school, and crank the heat right up to make sure I stepped onto the curb dripping in sweat. I would scream in frustration, then laugh so hard I couldn't breathe. Donnie made sure I never took myself too seriously. He also taught me to keep my cool, no matter what. This particular truth has come full circle many, many times. In so many situations where I might have been freaking out inside, I took a deep breath and stayed calm on the surface. No way was I going to let them see me flustered. Oh! That's why I had a big brother who picked at me so much. He was giving me grit. Ah-ha!

Meeting my first investor, Shana Fisher, was another ah-ha moment. So many unlikely events lined up perfectly to make that connection for me, and even when I resisted because I was so focused on the here and now, taking care of my kids and shipping out orders as fast as I could produce them, Shana pursued me. God was giving me chance after chance to finally get it. He wasn't going to give up until I got the message that it was time to be mentored and grow, both as a business owner and as a human being. He wasn't going to allow me to stay down in survival mode. Ah-ha!

More recently, when I was mandated to hire outside executives who I came to believe were wasting millions of dollars and killing revenue streams at Lolly Wolly Doodle, I couldn't comprehend why it was happening. I wanted to walk away and go back to selling things from my garage. But, when I fought back for control of the company, I finally understood. God was teaching me that I needed to stand up for what I believe in. He wanted to test me, so that I would finally get the fact that I was meant to be here. Until then, I thought I was in this position through some kind of fluke. Going through that challenge taught me to trust myself as a business leader. It also taught me that this was no longer just about me. I was just a part of something much, much bigger. I had 150 workers with families whose livelihoods depended on Lolly Wolly Doodle's survival. Beyond that, the culture of giving back that we created within our company affects our customers, our community, even villages halfway across the world. Ah-ha!

Ah-ha moments can be miracles, even if it doesn't seem like it at the time. No experience is ever wasted. Our biggest failures and tragedies teach us something. When I lost my beloved fiancé, Frannie, it seemed so random and unfair. Lord knows, if you had told me back then that it was a blessing, I'd have bitten your head off. But years later I feel nothing but pure gratitude that he was in my life, even if that time was cut short. Loss was the gift. It taught me resilience, humility, compassion, and opened me up to a relationship with God I never had before. It made me better in countless ways.

Ah-ha moments are life's big and little takeaways that lift you from one level to the next, if you let them. You can't make the ah-ha moment happen, but you can learn to pay more attention and tune in to what is going on within and around you to reap the benefits. Start by looking back on those turning points to connect the dots of those life lessons, and I promise you'll start seeing them all the time, and just when you need them the most.

The ah-ha moment comes when it's supposed to. Allow yourself to question it, but be okay when you don't have an immediate answer. There are some things I may never understand, and I am completely fine with that. They are just blessings that haven't ripened yet. When I walk through the pearly gates, I know I am going to have a lot of questions, but I trust that I'll find out, eventually. God has a sense of humor, that's for sure. The worst things will happen at the worst possible moment, and when I look back at those times with enough distance and perspective, it can be hysterical. But God is teaching me something, and it's up to me to make the most of every single experience He has in store for me.

Trusting in this higher wisdom is key. It opens you up to the flow of life. It frees you to let go of the resentments and disappointments of the past to make the most of the blessings and knowledge that can come your way every day if only you are present enough to notice. Too many people get so stuck in a notion of how things are supposed to be that they miss out on the miracle of possibilities and never move forward. They cling to their checklists and assume that circumstances have to be just so before they can take a step. As a result, they get in their own way.

This is especially true in business. So many executives and managers allow their methods and protocols to overrule common sense and kill creative thinking. They rely on the experts and tell themselves there is just one way to build a company. If Lolly Wolly Doodle did that, we wouldn't exist.

The ah-ha moment is when you are humble enough to acknowledge that you don't have all the answers.

The ah-ha moment is when you listen, I mean truly listen, to others and allow ideas to come through from some of the unlikeliest of places.

The ah-ha moment is when you stop looking in the rear-view mirror at all those past wrongs and disappointments.

The ah-ha moment is when you find a problem and persist until you solve it.

The ah-ha moment is when you permit yourself to experiment.

The ah-ha moment is when you allow yourself to fail. *Especially* when you fail.

The ah-ha moment is when you take a leap and find out that you have wings.

That's right. You can't just sit on your behind and wait for it to happen. You have to *do* something. So many people sit back and think God is going to do it all for them. I love blonde jokes. One of my favorites is about a blonde who found herself floating on the ocean in a raft after her ship sank. She prayed and prayed, "Lord, please save me!" The coast guard came by and offered to help, but she said no thank you. A helicopter hovered over and threw down a rope. "No, no, God's going to save me," she said. Eventually she drowned. When she got to heaven, she said, "God, I kept waiting on you!" He said, "Well, I sent the coast guard, I sent a helicopter. There is only so much I can do if you won't even help yourself!"

Most of all, the ah-ha moment is when you realize that you can take action and help yourself again, and again and again. You never have to be a victim of circumstances when you can hit that reset button. We get stuck in the mind-set that we only have one shot at success or happiness and the moment it goes wrong we are done. But my life is proof positive that there is no limit to the number of do-overs you get. That is God's greatest gift to all of us. AH-HA!

But you have to take action. You can't be passive. You have to reach forward and hit that thing! Let God help you by helping yourself. We have to trust that He is going to make a way, but we have to be ready and awake for it. We have to be willing to put in the work. Hitting the reset button is like saying, *Okay, I'm ready for whatever it is you have in store for me, and I'm gonna keep on trying.*

Listen, I know it's hard. If you're like most of us, you've probably had a belly full of failures, disappointments, and loss. I hear from moms who are going through unimaginable hardships every day. But you have to believe that what seems incomprehensible now will ultimately make perfect sense. Hang in there. It's going to come full circle. That messy divorce happened because you were meant to be with someone else. That job you lost was because you were supposed to move to a different city and build a life and career that you find truly fulfilling. That child with special needs was born to you because you were supposed to learn unconditional love and set an example for everyone around you.

It's my hope that, if you get just one ah-ha moment from this book, it's that you realize your potential is limitless. Those do-overs just keep coming. Being a victim, blaming the circumstances instead accepting them as unripened blessings, is the one sure way to close yourself off from something miraculous. So knock it off! Have the humility to acknowledge that you don't know all the answers. When you accept this fact, life gets a whole lot easier. And hang in there. If there's a silver lining to the hard, hard chapters of my earlier life, it's that all of it led me here, to the incredibly privileged position of being able to tell my story—every last detail of it–and by doing so, reach out a hand to you and say, "Hey, sister. It's Brandi here."

On these next pages I'm going to share with you my whole story: the successes, the failures, the embarrassments, and all the raw emotions of love, anger, gut-wrenching grief, heart-in-throat joy, and side-splitting laughter. No filters here. You'll learn about the birth of my business, its many growing pains, the role of my beloved yet eccentric family, and the people and relationships at the Doodle that make it so special. I'll describe the moment it was nearly all taken away, and the David and Goliath battle we fought to take it all back. I'll share with you all the challenges of this ongoing journey, and why I continue do it despite the heartache I experience as a mother juggling to make precious time for my kids while running a business that so often requires my 24/7 attention. Drawing lessons from these struggles and experiences, I'll flash back to the ordinary and extraordinary moments of my past that influenced me most and made me the woman I am today.

My story isn't linear and neither is life. It's been a roller coaster of ups, downs, gravity-force starts, and screeching halts. There are times when I need to take a moment and press pause before I hit reset. I need to stop and reflect on how I got here before I take that next big loop the loop. So buckle up for the ride and prepare to be entertained!

We're the same, you and I. You are a mom who stays at home with your kids or a woman who works two jobs to make ends meet but has ideas in her mind that she can't imagine ever pursuing. You might be young and just starting out, or maybe you are older and facing the fact that your kids no longer need as much from you. Whether out of need or desire, the question looms: What now? You are filled with shoulds, musts, and what-ifs. You think that if you want to start a business, you need to read a dozen how-to business books or maybe go back to school. To you I want to say what one of my angel investors said to me during a meeting: "Thank God you never read a business book, Brandi. Otherwise you never would have done this."

I broke the rules without knowing I was breaking them. In fact, in these years that Lolly Wolly Doodle has grown so enormously, some of my biggest mistakes have been made by listening to the experts. I've come to understand that the reason my business turned out to be so successful is because it wasn't a business—not in its conception. I wasn't strategizing, marketing, planning. It was plain old-fashioned common sense combined with a genuine connection to the customer. I was solving a problem. A very simple problem. My kids needed clothes. We needed extra cash. I used whatever was available to me. Every single scrap.

I've been scrappy ever since I can remember. In the South, when people hear that word, they think of someone who's always getting into fights. That's not me. Well, not unless I have to. But there's another definition: someone who uses everything they've got, every available resource, even something most people would overlook. Scrappy is the mom who has run out of grocery money and finds whatever she's got left in the fridge to make a delicious casserole to feed her family. Or the entrepreneur running her jewelry business on a shoestring and sourcing items from thrift shops and flea markets. You know, the person who sees possibility where others see the impossible and manages to create something out of nothing.

You don't have to wait for all the conditions to be perfect. You don't need an investor from *Shark Tank*. You don't need to live in a big city or have a fancy business degree. If you have an idea, just roll up your sleeves and act upon it. Even if you don't have an idea yet, listen closely to what your heart is telling you, hear the ah-ha's, then use your God-given common sense to make it happen. You'll make plenty of mistakes and suffer all kinds of setbacks, but that's okay. Failure is always an option if it teaches you how to do better next time, when you hit reset again.

I'm just like you, and I'm going to tell it to you straight. Let go of your lists. Stop thinking you can't or shouldn't. Or that it's impossible. Or that life doesn't work that way. Find a problem or a need—and there are plenty around—then figure out how to solve it. Whether it's building a business, finding a job you love, or creating a family, you were meant for something great. Now let me help you get there.

Love, Brandi

One

Press the Reset Button

You are never too old to set another goal or to dream a new dream.

–C. S. LEWIS

The mailman staggered up our driveway carrying a huge box covered in strange-looking postmarks and addressed to me. I'd been waiting on this shipment of girls' dresses from Shenzhen, China, for weeks, and I was as excited as a little kid at Christmas as I grabbed a pair of scissors from one of the sewing tables and slashed open the cardboard. As I dug past the layers of protective plastic and Styrofoam peanuts to pull out one of the smocked dresses I'd designed, I held my breath.

Customers on eBay had already been buying up my clothes as fast as I could sew them. My mom, my dad, my aunt, my nieces, a couple of ladies from my church, and my husband, Will, all helped out, and we got so big that we had to move from a corner of my bedroom to the garage. One day I had the idea that maybe I could outsource some of the sewing, so I went on Alibaba.com, a website I trusted, and found a manufacturer in China who said she could do it.

I'd always wanted to do a line of those cute smocked dresses, which use embroidery to gather material in an intricate honeycomb pattern to give a garment some flounce and stretch. It's a technique they used in the Old South back in the days before elastic was invented, and I thought it was an adorable, classic look. But they cost a fortune in the high-end baby boutiques, and you couldn't find these styles anywhere else. I knew this because I'd been searching high and low for my own daughters.

But if something doesn't exist on the market, why not make it yourself? If it's missing, it may be an opportunity. I knew that if I could produce some at an affordable price, not more than fifty dollars apiece, mothers like me would scoop them up. They were perfect for church and special occasions. It could fill a hole in the market and give me the kind of brand extension I was looking for without having to physically sew them myself.

Although I wasn't acknowledging it out loud, Will had already taken a couple of pay cuts, and I was beginning to think we needed a backup plan. There was only so much of me, so why not grow the business with a product I could just purchase as is? Besides, smocked garments were beyond my skill set. If I could test the market with something ready to ship, making an initial run with a small but affordable batch, we might get a nice boost to our household income.

I like to test out a theory, on a manageable scale. So I did my research the way I always do, on Google. Typing in keywords like "garment," "factory," and "China" led me to Alibaba.com, one of the world's biggest online commerce companies, which helped me find this woman, the Chinese factory manager, on the other side of the world. I sent her dozens of fabric photos, specs, and a money order—I actually sent her a $3,000 money order through Western Union, because I didn't know that this is generally a terrible idea. It was the minimum amount they would accept. When the shipment arrived (a small miracle that it arrived at all) it was all wrong.

One of the neckline prints was supposed to be black zebras on a pink background. The zebras looked like cows. And the measurements were off. Sleeves were different lengths, neck holes and armholes were too tight. The whole thing was a mess. My small clothing business was a thrifty operation, and I reinvested everything I earned back into necessities like bolts of fabric, so $3,000 was a huge amount of money to lose. But how would I recoup the loss? I didn't want to put these botched clothes on my eBay store since you live and die by customer reviews. I took a chance and I blew it. I felt sick about it, as if I'd let down my whole family.

But there was no time to dwell. It was October and we were ramping up for the holidays, our busiest time of year. I had my regular orders to fill, as well as the Junior League shows to attend all over South Carolina, North Carolina, and Georgia. So I shoved the box into a corner of the garage and tried to forget about it, although I shuddered with disgust whenever I walked past it. I hated being reminded of my failure. I'm the girl who likes to win.

Nothing to Lose

Finally, the Christmas rush was over. It was early in the morning of New Year's Eve 2009, when the rest of the family was still in bed and all was quiet around the house. It gave me time to think and, I must admit, throw myself a very small and exclusive pity party. You know how it is when you take stock of your life when another year is coming to a close? It's that dead zone between Christmas and the New Year when the presents are opened, the leftovers are eaten, and everything is still.

How did I end up here? I asked myself. *Why does my life always have to be such a struggle?*

Then a little voice inside me whispered, "Just try."

I started looking around the garage to see what else there was to sell. I figured I'd start off 2010 with a clean slate and clear out whatever leftover inventory I could, to at least recover the investment. Money was even more tight than usual, as we tend to go all out to celebrate the holidays. Any spare cash had been spent on gifts and toys, so every scrap had to count. Then my eyes fell on that box from China. It suddenly occurred to me to post pictures of those dresses on Facebook.

I didn't know much about social media. I didn't even realize that was what platforms like Facebook were called. But my cousin and best friend Ashley had been bugging me for months to set up a page on the site, so that I could see friends from high school and college.

"Are you kidding me?" I asked her. "You know I don't have time to play around on the computer."

But after hearing more about how many friends she was connecting with through the site, a light went on in my head. Maybe what was true for Ashley could be true for moms like me, so I decided to set up a business page. It might be a good way to keep up with all the ladies I met at the Junior League shows.

I'd only recently given my business, such as it was, a name. We'd nicknamed one of my nieces "Lolly" as a toddler because she was so grumpy the only thing that made her smile was when my grandfather, Pappaw, brought her lolly-pops. Then she'd squeal with delight. The day I started my eBay store, Lolly was sitting beside me and asked, "What are you going to call it, Aunt Brandi?"

"Oh I don't know. How about Lolly Wolly Doodle?" I joked.

It stuck. I only found out later that the name also sounds like an old children's song, "Polly Wolly Doodle":

Oh I went down South
For to see my Sal
Sing Polly Wolly Doodle all the day

Yep, I don't know what it means either. But somehow this quirky name, which I came up with almost by accident, suggests childhood innocence, something I was trying to recapture with the clothes I was making.

And that's as far as I got when it came to branding or marketing my dresses until a few weeks before the China fiasco, when I set up a Lolly Wolly Doodle page. I created it simply to let people know when I'd next be in their area for a Junior League show and to engage with a few of the moms I'd met on those sales trips. So why not let those same customers see the smock dresses and buy them at a discount? I described exactly what sizes I had, and what was wrong with them, then priced them at $15 each. If people wanted them, I'd ask them to write their address on my Facebook wall. I knew how to use PayPal, so I could invoice them via e-mail. At most, I thought, I might be able to recoup some of that $3,000. No harm in trying.

First, I put up the pink and black cow zebras. Then I walk away from the computer to grab a Diet Dr. Pepper from the kitchen. I hadn't taken more than a couple of steps before I started hearing a sound I would become very familiar: *ding* . . . *ding* . . . *ding.*

What in the world is that? I wondered.

I walked back to the computer and saw twenty orders on my Facebook feed.

"I'll take a size 8, here is my e-mail address. . . ." "I'll take a size 4. . . ." Each comment was an order. I thought I might sell a few of the dresses over the course of a few days, but those silly mutant zebra dresses sold out in a matter of minutes! I did a screenshot of the Facebook wall so that I could figure out how many orders I had and where to send them. Then I started sending PayPal invoices to each customer. To my surprise, each one paid right away.

More orders started pouring in. I couldn't understand it, because my page only had 152 likes. What I did not realize was that, back then, when someone made a comment, it would show up all over their friends' newsfeeds, and so on, and so on.

People who had never even heard of Lolly Wolly Doodle were seeing it for the first time and liking it. I watched as our number of fans grew to 200, then 300, then 500 in the space of a few days. And these were the irregular clothes from China!

The next day I decided to put up the other two smocked styles, a pink one with Scottie dogs around the neckline, and the other with a green and pink circle neckline. They were snapped up in seconds. Then I pulled out a box of really cute clothes left over from my last Christmas show, and put up some more photos. *Ding . . . ding . . . ding.* There it was again. It sounded like a slot machine hitting the jackpot, only much, much better. Something was happening here. I wasn't sure how, or why, but it was one of those moments when you know you are getting another chance.

Do-Over or Die

No matter how hard or complicated life gets, you can always press the reset button. We all can. Life is hard, and it isn't fair. You don't get rewarded just because you're a decent person, and you don't get time off for good behavior. **But the good news is that you are never out of options and you don't have to stay stuck in one identity, because there is no limit to the number of do-overs you can have.** It doesn't have to begin and end with the route you've already mapped out for yourself.

Think of it this way. When you are driving somewhere, you enter the address in your car's GPS system and follow the directions. But then you decide to stop for a sandwich.

You can choose to set this location either as a new destination or a stop on the way. The system accommodates and recalculates, because you are allowed to take detours. The journey is fluid. You can even change your mind about exactly where you would like to end up.

I have had to press the reset button multiple times in my life. It's gotten to the point where I can visualize that big red Staples button in my head, and knowing it's always there has given me hope in the darkest of times.

I pressed the reset button in college, when over the course of three years I switched majors three times. Growing up I'd always seen myself as some globe-trotting hotshot executive, so at first I studied prelaw with a concentration in Japanese and a minor in accounting. But I kept finding more interesting subjects, like marketing and interior design. I hit reset again after I married way too early and found myself in an unhealthy relationship and got divorced. I pressed it again after I spent a few years partying and being arm candy to a man old enough to be my father. I pressed it again when I fell for Fran, the father of my second child. I had to press it long and hard after Fran died, and I never thought I'd be whole again. I pressed it when, at twenty-nine, I found myself lost and devastated, and through the cracks in my heart, a small light of faith and hope began to shine through. I pressed it yet again when I got married to Will and we brought our two complicated families together. And I pressed reset once more when it turned out not to be a fairy-tale ending–when Will's job started falling apart, he was unhappy and angry, we were fighting, our baby was crying all the time, divorce absolutely was not an option, we were poised to lose everything, and I thought, uh-oh, here we go again. Finally, I pressed it the day I started cutting and sewing A-line patterns.

We get locked into this idea that you only get one opportunity to make it in life, that you have to be great at one thing, or that a first impression is the only one that matters. But the universe is infinite, and so are its possibilities. **God gives us as many chances as we are willing to take. If I didn't believe this, I would not be where I am today.** I wouldn't be CEO of my own company and blazing a trail in retail. I'd be bitter, broke, and looking back at my past as a series of disappointments. I'd be well and truly stuck.

Golden Girly Girl

I'd hate to be held to some of my earliest ambitions. In high school all I wanted in life was to become a trophy wife and maybe get that law degree on the side or something, just in case the trophy thing didn't work out so well. Even as a little girl, I was driven, but not in a career kind of way. In school I just wanted to be the best at everything, whether it was cheerleading, trendsetting, or making the honor's list. I was a princess, and I had this fantasy of my life as a jet-setter. Never in my wildest dreams did I think I would stay in Lexington, North Carolina.

"I can't wait to leave this Podunk town," I told my father one day, when I was still in middle school.

Daddy was a hardworking, salt-of-the-earth brick mason, and he doted on me. When he was off work for a bad back and my mother was at her administrative job at a local school, he'd come up to my bedroom and have pretend tea parties or play postman with me in my closet. We must have been quite a sight, this big, burly man and his towheaded toddler. He'd have done anything to make my wishes come true.

"Well, if that's what you want, baby, you'll get it. I know you will," he told me. "You can do anything you put your mind to."

My parents were my biggest enablers. Growing up, I never doubted myself, and in many ways that was a good thing, because it made me fearless. They didn't spoil me, exactly. I was expected to study hard and work to earn any extras, and Mom regularly blessed me out for giving her attitude or failing to do what she asked of me. But, thanks to the way my mother and father raised me, it didn't even occur to me that my dreams weren't possible. They had a good, if not perfect, marriage and provided a loving and stable home for my brothers and me. Even though we were poor—my father's health issues meant there were a few years with little to no income—I never felt deprived. I grew up with a silver-plated spoon in my mouth and was always encouraged to aspire to more in life.

We weren't exactly the Cleavers. A streak of crazy runs through my DNA on both sides. Daddy always had a fierce temper, not that I was ever on the receiving end, and my mother could be compulsive about a lot of things. She was a hoarder, and our house was always stuffed to the rafters with whatever crafts she was obsessed with at the time. (One year it was pecan figurines, another it was doll houses.) She got her eccentricities from her mother, Betty, my best friend and partner in crime well into my teen years.

Mammaw Betty was a classic Southern belle, but she was certifiable. Her husband, my pappaw, was the sweetest, gentlest man on earth, but it got so bad one time that he hit her with a two-by-four and put her in the hospital. Of course, this was all information I gathered later on in life. My early years were spent in a protective bubble, mostly oblivious of the dysfunction. I was the golden-haired girly girl my parents had waited for, and as the baby of the family I got the best that they could give.

I had two brothers–Donnie, who is nine years older than me, and Patrick, the middle child, who is six and a half years my senior. They fought with each other constantly, with their fists and any other objects lying around the house. Daddy finally bought them each a pair of boxing gloves and insisted they duke it out when things reached the boiling point, which was a twice-weekly event at least. Donnie usually won, but Patrick would find ways to get even. After one pummeling, Patrick snuck onto the roof and pushed a chunk of ice onto Donnie's head, knocking him unconscious. When Daddy had enough he'd thrash their behinds raw with his Bassmaster belt. It wasn't abuse exactly–more like old-school discipline. But as much as my brothers got on each other's nerves, if anyone else tried to hurt one, they'd have the other to answer to. As we say in the South, family first.

And that's how they were with me. Donnie used to tease me without mercy. He called me "Little Miss Prisspot." Knowing how competitive I was and how much I wanted to be first at everything, he made it his mission to keep me down to earth. Lord help me if I got too big for my lacy britches. But my brothers always looked out for their baby sister. They were as proud as could be when I made all the school honor's lists. Everyone in the family got a kick out of the fact that I'd made it into a local cheerleading squad as a mascot by the age of five. Patrick and Donnie secretly delighted in the fact that I won all these local beauty pageants. When I was crowned homecoming queen and Miss Barbecue Festival the very next day (pit-cooked pig is the local delicacy), Patrick grumbled that he had to drive me down Lexington's main street in the local parade, but he was grinning ear to ear. Of course, my old college roommates call me "Miss Piggy" to this day.

Pepto-Bismol Pink

Daddy was less pleased when I decided I had to be first among my friends to get married. I'd just come home for summer break after being away at school, Appalachian State, where I had big plans to study law and Japanese, thinking that would get me access to some glamorous corporate job. My mother asked me to help out by serving sodas at a trade show for the pneumatic company where she was bookkeeping, and introduced me to the owner's son, Eric, a cute guy who'd just joined the police academy. We hit it off and I liked him a little bit, but I especially liked the idea of being a police officer's wife. Above all, I loved the possibility of planning an extravagant wedding, complete with eleven bridesmaids in dresses the color of Pepto-Bismol pink. It was a scene straight out of *Steel Magnolias*.

I continued going to college in the evenings and working for Eric's dad during the day, to supplement my husband's

$16,000 a year salary. It was fun being married to a handsome policeman, and women were always making passes at him. This time it felt like I was the one with the trophy. We built a cookie-cutter house beside my parents' home, and, within five months of being married, the day before my twenty-first birthday, I found out I was pregnant.

I also found out that my picture-perfect marriage wasn't all that it seemed. My whole world came crashing down around me. I felt ashamed. I was an honors student, destined to see the world, and I gave it all up for a husband I believed adored me. I stuck it out until a couple of years after my son, Kade, was born, going through a roller coaster of couples counseling and emotional turmoil until I couldn't take it anymore. My white picket-fence dream turned to dust. First one to get married, pregnant, and divorced. As a young single mother and college dropout who wasn't getting a dime in child support, I was done with being first.

Arm Candy

Then I hit that reset button hard. ***The thing about having your back against a wall is that there's no time to check items off your wish list or linger over past regrets. You just do what you must to get your life back on track.*** I had my son to support, so I landed a job on the sales team at one of world's largest furniture stores. Furniture happens to be one of North Carolina's biggest industries, and, although it was never one of my ambitions, I discovered I had a talent not just for selling big-ticket items but for interior design.

Soon I was making six figures and traveling all over the East Coast, decorating homes for celebrities, dating pro athletes, and rubbing elbows with the rich and famous from Boston to West Palm Beach. Eric had been a lousy husband, but he was a great father, and we had shared custody, so on my weeks without Kade I indulged my new fancy: to be arm candy for a wealthy older businessman and live the dream of private jets, luxury vacations, and a designer wardrobe.

Those years between my early and mid-twenties were my chance to sow a few oats and make up for all the fun I missed by starting a family so young. I loved being pursued, adored, and spoiled rotten. Hanging out with movers and shakers opened my eyes to the world outside of sleepy ole Davidson County. I met Max, my first sugar daddy, a sophisticated bachelor old enough to be my father who would fly me in to New York, where he had an office, and set me up with a personal shopper at Saks Fifth Avenue. After my first trip to New York, in 1998, I came back dressed in tall boots, a miniskirt, a cute little hat, and sunglasses—all in black. It was way before anyone else wore that look, years ahead of Lexington, and I couldn't wait to show off. I stopped by the local barbecue joint where I knew my dad was having his lunch with his construction friends and did a twirl. He howled with laughter.

"That's my girl! This is what we've been expecting from you your whole life!"

But it got old. Once the novelty of this jet-set lifestyle wore off, it just seemed empty. I grew bored with Max and all the other eligible men who chased, fawned, and put me on a pedestal. It was time for another reset, only this time it wasn't a conscious choice. I fell in love.

Cracked Open

I met Fran Papasedero, coach of the Orlando Arena Football League team, entirely by accident. I was already starting to date a handsome young doctor in town and was toying with the idea of a new identity as a doctor's wife when a girlfriend asked me to join her for drinks with these two sports guys who were in town on a consulting gig. She'd intended to set me up with Fran's friend, but neither of them was my type. Fran was a mountain of a man with muscles on muscles. What he had left of his hair was flame red, another immediate turn-off. And he was obnoxious. Within minutes of our meeting he took obvious delight in picking at me. He was hilarious and annoying at the same time, and before long I couldn't resist.

Fran was unlike any other man I'd ever met. From the start he saw right through me and called me on my BS. This man knew exactly what buttons to push. I never laughed so hard or lived so fully until I met him. Before long I found my-self accidentally pregnant with my second child, Vivian, and broken up with Fran, her father. We didn't reunite until Vivi was born. Soon I found myself indefinitely engaged and com-muting back and forth between my home in Lexington and Fran's condo in Orlando. My universe revolved around this larger-than-life character.

Then my life imploded. Just as we were talking about

setting a date for our wedding, Frannie was killed in a drunk driving accident. For the next several months I was buried under an avalanche of grief, but I had to press reset again. What other choice did I have? Our daughter together was three years old. By the time I was twenty-nine, I had lived several lives, had two little kids to prove it, and had nothing to my name. I mean to say, I had a blue minivan, which we called the Smurf, and $700 to my name. I'd given up my job and my home in Lexington because Frannie was going to take care of us. But there was no insurance money. Fran lived large and spent what he made enjoying life. Even the condo we occupied wasn't owned by him; it belonged to the team.

Recalculating

With a road full of painful wreckage behind me, I was back home in Lexington—the last place in the world I ever wanted to end up. I had no child support from either of my children's fathers. I needed to work and figured I could do acrylic nail training, a skill I'd picked up while living in Orlando and working in a salon part-time. I was tired and grieving—and in my devastation, I was somehow broken open. I had spent my whole life wanting to be first, wanting to get ahead. First to get married. First to have a baby. First to have a sugar daddy. First to be a trophy wife. First to have a house and a nice car. I was always crossing things off lists. Now, there was no list. Nothing to cross off. Just me, taking a good hard look at myself and how in my rush to be first I had lost sight of everything that mattered.

I met my current husband, Will–a single dad with a son–and after dating for a while we started going to church together. This time it was about building an adult relationship based on mutual faith and real partnership. Eventually we blended our two families and had another baby together–our daughter, Eva Bella. Finally, life seemed to be on track. Except if there's one thing I know, it's that there's no such thing as life being on track. It's full of stops, starts, and detours. Eva Bella was an incredibly difficult baby who never–literally never–stopped crying. I hadn't been physically well during my pregnancy with her, and so I was feeling less than my usual bounce-back-to-it self. And as the full effect of the mortgage crisis closed in, Will started worrying about his job stability.

I was afraid, once again, and knew that I needed to step up and do something to support our family, at least in the short term. But I had no idea what. Years earlier, Mammaw Betty, an expert seamstress, had taught me how to sew, so I decided to dust off my rudimentary skills and sew some of my own kids' clothes, both to save money and because I didn't like what was out there. One day I bought a little too much fabric and decided to use the leftovers–not quite scraps, but close to it–to make a few more outfits to sell to other moms I knew in our community. I loved the way a monogram looked on children's clothes and thought, *I can do that.* The requests for more personalized clothes started pouring in.

Look around you and use whatever you've got. It's what Daddy, Mom, and Mammaw imprinted on me long ago, so that's what I did. I dug deep within myself to solve a problem and, determined to be scrappy and recycle, got to work.

I kept it really simple: A-line dresses for girls and long johns for boys. I started selling them at street festivals around North Carolina. Those street festivals eventually led to Junior League holiday shows. The children's clothes were all about the way I wanted to see my own kids dressed: wholesome, modest, and like kids—not like little mini-me versions of their moms. It was all sweet and colorful with lots of patterns and appliqués, and always monograms, done right on the spot. People seemed to really love the clothes, so I started a small eBay store. I saw what I was doing as extra cash for my weekly visits to the nail salon. Or, at the most, as a way of shoring up our finances until my husband's salary got better.

Going Viral

Then I got that fateful notion to have smock dresses made in China. The day after that first posting, I grabbed every item of children's clothing I could lay my hands on. I wanted to test the theory that, if the flawed garments got snapped up, these same Facebook fans—ladies I'd met at the Junior League shows as well as their friends and friends of friends—would not be able to get enough of the items that were actually made to my much higher standards.

I pulled whatever I could find off the shelves and out of boxes and photographed each dress, bloomer, jumper, and top against the brick wall outside our garage. The lighting was perfect, and the night-light fixture provided a handy place for me to hang up each garment. I moved quickly, ironing, steaming, snapping, cropping, and posting one item after another. It was so much faster than posting on eBay, which could take twenty minutes to get something nicely listed, complete with pretty backgrounds and full descriptions. It was so labor intensive that the most I could do was five or six items a day. But on Facebook I could post dozens.

Then Lolly Wolly Doodle started showing up in the Facebook feeds of all these women's friends, and a flood of customers joined our page. The numbers swelled from hundreds to thousands, and I couldn't stop smiling. I still wasn't sure if this was beginner's luck or something more, but it was definitely an ah-ha moment. I was onto something. This was big.

That night, when Will got home from work, I told him what was happening.

"Honey, you're not going to believe this, but I think we may have won the lottery."

"Huh? Are you teasing me?"

"No, really, look!" I said, showing him the Facebook wall, which was filling up with comments as fast as I could hit the refresh tab.

"I don't know if I am supposed to do this on Facebook," I told him. "I'm not sure how it works."

I Googled and learned enough to understand that the rules at the time were fuzzy. But it was enough to let me justify what I was doing, because I sure as heck didn't want to stop. As my grandmother used to say, "Can they eat you?" They may have found out and shut me down, but in the meantime we were making cold, hard cash. When I told him what I learned, Will was all for it.

"Well then, it's a blessing," he said. "Praise the Lord and be happy about it. Keep doing what you are doing and let's get rid of all this stuff!"

Healthy Addiction

Over the next several days and weeks, it was trial and error. I was driving myself crazy sending out individual invoices. There were so many customers I'd forget who bought what and have to look at my notes. I finally got smart and realized I could put the item and size number in the subject line. I figured out all of the things I needed to do to make the process go faster.

It became an addiction. Posting a little dress or a romper was the drug, and the Facebook frenzy was the high. Within seconds of putting up an A-line dress, forty people would want to buy it. I was constantly wondering how I could get more to post, and faster. I even raided Bella and Vivi's closet for outfits they'd never worn.

"You're never going to wear these, are you?" I'd ask them.

"Well, yeah, maybe," they said.

"Ah, come on! It's been hanging there for two months untouched. Let me sell it."

"Probably not. Okay. . . ."

And before they could change their minds I was halfway down the stairs.

From Hobby to Business

Once those first twenty invoices were paid, I had enough money to buy a whole bolt of fabric. I used the rest of the proceeds to hire more people to cut and sew quickly. Suddenly, my hobby had turned into a business, and within two weeks I took down the eBay store to concentrate full-time on Facebook. Because I didn't yet have a whole lot of items to sell, I announced that I would post new items at 9 p.m. It seemed like the ideal time for moms to go online shopping, when dinner was made, kids were bathed and put to bed, and they could sit in front of their computers with a glass of chardonnay and a credit card within reach. Even if they were early to bed, there was just enough time after the witching hour to have a little fun.

After I got everyone in the habit of being ready at nine, it became a kind of game to them. At 8:45, people would start posting:

"Who all is on here? Anyone I know?"

They'd start talking back and forth, saying:

"Oh my gosh, I'm soooo nervous."

"I can't wait."

"I got all my information saved and all I have to do is hit the button and paste."

"I'm gonna win tonight!"

It was such a competition I didn't even know if they cared what I was selling. They were fighting over these limited items, and the fact that they were so scarce and their friends wanted them too made them crazy. Once the first post was up, my brother Donnie would get on the phone with me, and we'd have the whole family on speaker, watching as the numbers went up and up and up.

"Wow, sis, look at that! You just got seventy-four comments in ten seconds!"

No matter what I put up, people bought it. Women even started creating fake accounts and squabbling with each other because their kids were the same size and they wanted the same dress.

The next thing that happened was that moms started posting photos of their own kids wearing our designs. A story began unfolding as I tried to deal with our rapid expansion. A mom posted a photo of the moment she brought her adopted daughter home from China—wearing Lolly Wolly Doodle. Another mom posted a photo of her baby son wearing Lolly Wolly Doodle to meet his dad for the first time when he came back from Afghanistan. A mom would post that her daughter had just been rushed to the hospital, and the other moms would offer prayers. Or a mom would ask if we had anything yellow and purple for her daughter's school dance.

The women bonded, the way moms do, and formed a community, and it was all happening on the Lolly Wolly Doodle Facebook page. I didn't even need to ask why. I knew, because these customers were just like me. It was all about the kids. The moms might have been wearing sweatshirts with holes in them, they might have had spit-up in their hair, but none of that mattered if someone came up to them in a restaurant and told them how adorable their daughter looked in that outfit. My Doodle fans took such pride in their children and wanted them to look cute and special—at a reasonable price.

Every Single Scrap

Years before, if anyone had told me this was going to happen, I would have laughed and said it was impossible. I hadn't done anything special. *I had done what I had spent my*

*whole life learning to do: making something out of
scraps and never quitting, finding a way, even when it
felt impossible to take another step.*

But that's how I became a CEO. I broke the rules without
knowing I was breaking them. I broke them with the same
tenacity of spirit I had when I was in the fifth grade and I
kept a notebook in which I wrote down every single thing I
wore each day so I wouldn't repeat the same outfit twice in
a month. My family had no money, but I knew intuitively how
to take whatever I had and make something of it. When that
shipment of irregular clothes came in from China, what
would have happened if I had simply thrown up my hands
and absorbed the loss? What if I had just given up? What
if I *hadn't* pressed reset? Well, I wouldn't be the CEO of a
company whose investors believed it could one day have a
billion-dollar valuation—one of the largest employers in Lexington, with two warehouses and office space adding up to
a hundred thousand square feet, and an office in New York
City for our tech and marketing team. That's for sure.

And God's timing could not have been more perfect. Not
long after the Facebook blowup, Will finally got notice that
he was about to lose his job and was juggling finances to make
our car and house payments. We were teetering on the brink
of losing it all. One evening after a particularly rough day at
work, he sat me down.

"Brandi there's something I have to tell you."

"What is it, honey?"

"We're about a month away from not being able to pay any
of our bills. We could lose our home, our car. . . ."

"Oh no, we're going to be fine," I told him.

There was more than enough money in the bank to cover our monthly expenses. I just had to keep doing what I was doing. From that moment on we agreed we'd switch roles. Another reset. Will would stay home and look after the kids while I turned my attention to running Lolly Wolly Doodle full-time, which was pretty much what I was already doing while being a stay-at-home mom.

If it happened to me, it could happen to you. Over the years I have met legions of women who have their fingers poised, ready to press their own reset button and take control of their lives—only they don't even know it yet. ***It's just a question of shifting your perspective and recalculating. You have to be willing to pivot and adapt to whatever challenges get thrown on your path.***

I'm a woman who used to care a lot about how things looked on paper—more than about how they actually felt. A woman who wasn't really living her life but was chasing after fantasies and crossing milestones off her list—as if life is a race to some sort of invisible finish line. I'm a woman who worshipped at the altar of unattainable perfection. Then real life brought me to my knees.

Since then, I've learned a lot about the difference between dreaming and doing. And the difference between being a slave to my impulses and following my deepest instincts. But all those other roads I traveled weren't dead ends. There is nothing wrong with taking the scenic route if it teaches you something. All those past identities of mine weren't just detours because, ultimately, they taught me lessons, sharpened my instincts, and gave me a better since of direction. They gave me countless ah-ha moments, which is why I don't re-gret a thing.

Of course hitting reset doesn't erase everything. It doesn't mean you don't have to deal with all the difficulties of your life anymore. ***It means that you make a conscious decision to start over, even if that means cleaning up pieces of what you're leaving behind, or recycling them in a whole new way.***

It floors me how many people tell themselves they are too old or too broke, too this or too that. People get ideas in their head, like, *Tomorrow I am leaving him and starting my life over*, and wake up the next day changing their minds because it's too hard. But you can hit reset in small, manageable ways, knowing it is not going to be for the last time. If you hate your job but need to stay because you have a family support, you can take small, practical steps toward finding a new way of earning a living, whether that's taking an evening class to improve your skill set or saving up a small financial cushion that buys you just enough time to execute your plan. It's just a question of visualizing that big red button. Once you've made that decision, you will find a path forward. You will get that do-over, each and every time.

AH-HA'S

- If something doesn't exist on the market, make it yourself. Where there is a gap, you may well find an opportunity.
- Just try. You can always minimize risk by putting something to the test on a manageable scale.
- You are never out of options. You don't have to stay stuck in one identity; there is no limit to the number of do-overs you can have.
- Having your back against a wall may be a blessing, because there is no time to check items off your wish list or linger over past regrets. You just do what you must to get your life back on track.
- Look around you and use whatever you've got. Dig deep within yourself to solve a problem.
- Sometimes it's a question of shifting your perspective and recalculating. You have to be willing to pivot and adapt to whatever challenges get thrown on your path.
- Make a conscious decision to start over, even if that means cleaning up pieces of what you're leaving behind, or recycling them in a whole new way.
- Reuse those scraps, and never quit. Keep searching for a way, even when it feels impossible to take another step.

Two

Embrace Blissful Ignorance

All you need in this life is ignorance and confidence, and then success is sure.

–MARK TWAIN

n a blazing hot summer morning in 2010 I was in full-blown mommy mode as I drove myself from Lexington to the airport in Charlotte, an hour and a half away. Wracked with guilt about abandoning my kids, even for a day, and panicked that I was completely unprepared for what lay ahead, I hadn't slept more than two hours the night before. I woke up just before dawn to lay out my kids' clothes, pack their lunches, and make sure they had everything they needed for all of their summer activities that day.

But what really sent me into a tailspin was what to wear. Working out of our garage got me out of the habit of looking polished. So much for my beauty queen days. T-shirts and yoga pants had become my uniform, and brushing my hair was an afterthought. I had to reach far back into my closet to dig up clothes from one of my more glamorous past lives. All I could find was a J. Crew blazer (so I'd look at least semi-professional) and the nicest (okay, the only) dress pants I owned. Eva Bella, my youngest, was four years old, and my older kids and step-son were ten, fifteen, and twenty-one, so I hadn't flown anywhere, much less to New York City, in a very long time.

In my purse was a ticket sent to me by a woman named Shana Fisher, a venture capitalist who had been calling me for months and months, asking me to come up and meet with her. She wanted to talk with me about Lolly Wolly Doodle, but to what end I didn't know. I'd been reluctant to make the trip because I was insanely busy—literally sewing dresses all night long and taking care of my kids. I kept putting her off until two things happened. First, I finally had a free moment to look this Shana Fisher up. It turned out she had been named one of the ten most powerful women on the Internet. Second, she sent me a ticket and promised me a driver would pick me up at LaGuardia, then swiftly return me after our meeting so I could be home with my family by dinnertime.

Busting at the Seams

By that time our business was exploding out of my garage. I was staying up all night, filling orders as fast as humanly possible. We were beyond the capacity of my church ladies and aunts. I had Will running the monogram machine and Daddy cooking dinner because we didn't even have time to feed ourselves. My helpers loved his spicy chicken stir-fry, barbecue beans, and potato soup. By this time Daddy's health was fail-ing quickly from heart disease and COPD, but he poured all his energy into making us his whole repertoire of hearty, stick-to-your-ribs, Southern soul food to keep us going. My mother-in-law, Nana Faye, liked to help out as well and occasionally treated us to one of her multilayered coconut cakes to fuel us through the rest of the night.

Soon I had to bring on a few employees to help because demand was overwhelming. I was consumed by the busi-ness and physically exhausted. My mother stayed up until four each morning doing invoices. We were doing round-the-clock shifts on those sewing machines, which took over the entire garage. We had dresses, baby bubbles, and bloomers hanging on racks in the dining room, foyer, and spare bedroom, which was piled high with blanks waiting to be customized. We were literally busting at the seams. But they didn't stay on the shelves for long. For every ten dresses we sold, there were three hundred people trying to buy them.

By March, just three months after the Facebook blowup, business had grown tenfold, and the cash had been flowing into our bank account nonstop. It seemed too good to be true, and I was scared to death that something would happen to ruin it. My husband had lost his job, we had all these kids, and all I wanted to do was avert disaster. I'd already had enough catastrophes in my life. I figured I should do some-thing with this bird in hand, this business that took me entirely by surprise. But every last ounce of energy I had was used up, and I hit a wall. So what I really had in mind was whether I might be able to sell Lolly Wolly Doodle for, like, a million dollars. It was a number I plucked out of thin air. It seemed like a lot.

I put some feelers out. ***Connections, even if it's a friend of a friend of a friend, are key. You'd be surprised who you can find when you ask around.*** Daddy and Donnie were friendly with a gentleman they took on their hog-hunting expeditions who became a coinvestor in their hunting club—Bond Isaacson. As it happens, Bond was a heavy hitter—a veteran financial executive who had been on the boards of several major corporations and had some deep connections in the investment community all over the world. It sure helped that he also liked to shoot things.

"I don't know of anyone looking to buy an apparel company, and I really don't think you should sell," he told me. "But I'd be happy to ask around."

Weeks later, shortly after we learned that Will was going to lose his job, I decided selling was no longer an option. It had to be our going concern, at least until the economy turned around and Will found another job. But that could be a while. The recession had hit Lexington especially hard, and the unemployment rate was about 14 percent. Everyone we knew in construction had been laid off, and we were out of options. Then I got a call from Bond.

"I know you don't want to sell anymore, but there is this lady in New York who is driving me nuts," he told me. "She keeps calling and e-mailing me for an introduction."

"Seriously? Why would someone in New York be interested in what I'm doing?"

"A friend of mine in New York told a few people, and they

told a few people. She looked you up and she is crazy about what you are doing."

What was I doing, and how could she possibly know anything about it? I wondered.

Bond forwarded me the e-mail thread and suggested I contact her myself. I could see from the back and forth that she was persistent. I Googled her and was stunned to learn what a powerhouse she was. I printed out her bio and ran to the kitchen to read it to Will.

"Can you believe someone like that would actually be interested in me?" I asked him.

"Well then, you better give her a call. See what she has to say."

So I dropped her a line, and she hit me back within minutes with her number.

"Please call me in ten minutes."

New York Angel

I went to the bathroom and shut the door. With kids running around and a screaming preschooler, it was the only quiet place in the house. I sat down against the tub with a notebook and pen in my hand, and dialed. When Shana picked up, she gushed:

"Hey, I am so happy you called. Do you realize what you've done? You've achieved the impossible. Everyone's been saying you can't build a business on Facebook and you've done it! Your stats are out of this world! I've been watching all the likes and comments on these pages over the past few days, and it's incredible! How did you come up with the idea?"

"Uh, thanks! I just had some stuff I needed to sell. Facebook was free and I knew how to do a PayPal invoice, so. . . ."

I wasn't sure how to tell Shana it was a total accident, that somehow God had blessed me with this new business, and the rest was just common sense. I hated to disappoint her.

"You have to come to New York. I have to meet you."

"I'm sorry, but I am just so busy and I really don't want to sell."

"No, no, don't sell! Do you hear me? Do not sell this company!"

She explained that she wanted to give me some capital to help me get the business to the next level. But I wasn't interested in her money. My understanding was that if you accept money from an investor, they either end up with equity, which amounts to partial ownership and control of your company, or you have to start paying them back right away, either in the form of interest or dividends. I didn't know there was such a thing as angel investors who were interested in helping you to build something long term.

But then she said something that intrigued me. She told me she could help me develop technology that I could plug in to make all that busy work of taking orders and invoicing automatic. My poor mother was getting tired. If there was something out there that could allow us to spend more time on creating products to sell and less on data entry, I was in. My mother wasn't the only one who needed a good night's sleep.

Never Let Them See You Sweat

I suffer from motion sickness, and it was a bumpy flight, so I was far from feeling my best by the time I landed at LaGuardia Airport. But there was something comforting about seeing my name on a sign at the bottom of the escalator, held up by a smiling bear of a man who introduced himself to me as "Blackjack" (you can't make this stuff up). He whisked me to a big black Mercedes with tinted windows and drove me into Manhattan, giving me a running commentary on the skyline and distracting me from my postflight nausea. As I sat in the back on those soft leather seats, surrounded by cut crystal glasses, designer water, and all the latest magazines, I started to feel better. I flashed back to those rides from hell in my big brother Donnie's '72 Gran Torino, tickled by the stark contrast and wishing he could see me now.

He used to pick me up covered head-to-toe in grease from the auto body shop where he worked. Of course, when I asked him to drop me off a block from where my friends were waiting for me, he did the exact opposite, pulling up right in front of them tooting his horn. If it was a hot summer day he'd crank up the heat on the passenger side, just to make me sweat. When he came to get me afterward, he'd drive to where I was standing, wait for me to reach for the door handle, then suddenly take off. He did this again and again, until I was breathless.

"Donnie Tysinger, why are you so mean to me!" I'd scream, in between fits of laughter.

Now it had come circle, and I knew exactly why. So I'd learn to never let them see me rattled. I could be outwardly calm no matter how much frenzy was going on beneath the surface. But this time I was more confused than nervous. I didn't even know why I was there. Why had this Shana woman chased after me so persistently? Why was she so excited to meet me? I didn't feel like I was doing anything special.

We pulled up to a modern all-glass look-at-me building in Manhattan's Chelsea neighborhood, and I was ushered into the enormous white contemporary space of IAC, Barry Diller's company, for my meeting. Digital art decorated the vast lobby floor to ceiling, and the reception area was covered with huge screens showing all the latest financial news. A New York City landmark designed by the world-famous architect Frank Gehry, it looked like a sleek and stylish spaceship—a far cry from the musty, mahogany-paneled offices with mounted heads of stags or bears I'd visited in Charlotte. I felt completely out of place.

Shana's flamboyant and impeccably groomed assistant greeted me. He reminded me exactly of Sean Hayes's character on *Will & Grace*. All teeth and smiles, yet completely genuine in his enthusiasm as he squealed, "Brandeeee! We're sooo excited you're here!!!"

And then I met Shana. I had been expecting someone who looked like Sigourney Weaver in *Working Girl*, but she was nothing like the corporate tiger I'd imagined. Instead, this venture capital whiz was an itty-bitty thing, just a hair over five feet tall and maybe a hundred pounds. She was friendly, down to earth, and had pictures of her young children all over her clean, crisp office. When I remarked on how cute they were, her face lit up. Then she explained that, since she had kids later in life, she wanted more balance in her life. The angel investor known for having the Midas touch stepped down from running Barry Diller's portfolio to focus more on family and start her own fund, investing in promising companies in their infancy, like mine. *Okay*, I thought, *at least we have something in common. She's also a mom.*

Shana had asked me to bring my business plan to the meeting. I didn't have a business plan, so I printed out a few pages of designs along with some photos of my own kids and their friends looking cute wearing them, and stuck the pages into one of those plastic homework folders Vivi had lying around the house. As we sat around a table in Shana's office, which had the most amazing floor-to-ceiling view of the Hudson River and the High Line, she started using terms that were completely foreign to me. EBIDTA. Conversion rate. Balance sheet. Spreadsheet....

She talked about engineers. *Why did we need engineers?* I wondered. She raved about how much potential she saw in my business. She said we had done what everyone considered impossible. She spoke matter-of-factly about studies and articles that had been written about monetizing social media—very much assuming that I was familiar with them. She called me a social media genius.

I didn't know what social media was.

After twenty minutes of nodding and pretending I had any idea what was going on, I realized she was talking about Facebook.

As embarrassed as I was about my lack of sophistication, there wasn't a shred of condescension in her voice. She told me that I'd achieved the impossible in building my business on Facebook's newsfeed. I had no idea why others weren't doing it or that it was some sort of e-commerce unicorn. She even gushed about our Lolly Wolly Doodle designs and how the next big thing in apparel would be personalization and customization.

"I've been looking for something unique in clothing, and yours are so fresh and different," she told me. "In New York we all try to be different but then you see a jacket and you just know it's J. Crew."

It was a hot summer day and it was warm in Shana's office despite the air conditioning, but I didn't dare remove my jacket, in case she saw the label. I felt even more exposed when she brought in her junior associate and they started talking numbers. Shana explained that she wanted to give me some money to "get me out of the garage." I was suspicious. There had to be a catch. Then they asked me how much I thought my company was worth.

"Uh, a million dollars?" I blurted. "But I'm not selling."

"How did you come up with that figure?"

I pulled out the school workbook and showed them my "spreadsheet"—a Word document that listed monthly sales and added them up. I put in tabs and lined up the numbers, and threw in a bank statement for good measure. I could tell by the looks they exchanged with each other that they were amused, but they made every effort not to make me feel stupid.

"I'm sorry, I guess this isn't what you need," I said.

"Well, do you have a P&L or an income statement? What are your net earnings?"

I had no clue what they were talking about, and they could tell. But based on the amount of cash I had sitting in the bank, the fact that my overheads were virtually nonexistent, and our designs were selling as fast as we could get them out the door, Shana agreed my seat-of-the-pants valuation was fair.

"Look, I don't want to buy your company for a million dollars," Shana said.

Her associate sat beside her taking notes. The conference table gleamed in the afternoon light through those dazzlingly panoramic windows.

"I want to *invest* in your company. I don't think you understand that you've completely cracked a code that no one else has been able to crack."

"So do you think my company might be worth $5 million some day?" I asked her. And she smiled a sweet, quizzical smile. "Brandi, if I thought your company was only going to be worth $5 million, we wouldn't be sitting here."

Falling Stars

Shana told me she believed we could easily build the business up to a $50 million valuation within a few short years. I almost fell out of my chair. I thought this brilliant woman must somehow have had me confused with someone else. In the car on the way back the airport, I replayed the meeting again and again in my mind, trying to understand what was happening. If you had told me that within the next two years we would go through two rounds of venture capital financing, and that by the end of that period our investors would give Lolly Woolly Doodle a potential valuation of a *billion* dollars, I would have laughed and told you that was impossible. From the beginning it felt like I was the one who just happened to get there first. The first falling star was that I figured it out, and executed quickly, before I could even process what was happening. The other falling star was that, through a friend of a friend, Shana found out about us and tracked me down.

This kind of thing just doesn't happen to people like me, I told myself. It was like a dream scenario. I was the girl next door made good. I hadn't done anything special. Truly! I had done what I had spent my whole life learning to do: making something out of scraps, and never quitting, finding a way, even when it felt impossible to take another step.

At first I was terrified to take Shana's money. She said she wanted to help me build the business, but what did that even mean? (Eventually she would invest $100,000 in my company as a gesture of her good faith, and when we went into our first round of venture capital meetings, that $100,000 was still untouched in my bank account.) As much as I trusted her, my history had taught me that life isn't fair. That bad things can and do happen. I had a family to support, and all I wanted was keep our heads above water.

But Shana had planted a seed that day. Ultimately, it was her advice and mentorship that would become far more valuable to me than any cash in the bank. Receiving the validation and respect of someone like her was another miracle. It taught me that what was happening in our garage wasn't just some bit of blind luck. Yes, God had blessed me, but our success wasn't random. It was the product of hard work and, frankly, not knowing any better. I had caught the attention of one of the most powerful people in venture capital because I had unintentionally "cracked the code" of selling on Facebook, something all the experts had sworn could not be done. But, had I been aware of this, I may never have tried.

Many successful entrepreneurs get their start by not knowing the limits. Understanding how things are supposed to be done can throw up false barriers and curb the imagination. Instead, I used the few resources I had to solve a problem, and the business world was amazed.

Masters of Grit

You don't have to have an MBA from Wharton to start a business. Later on in this book you'll hear about how some of the most impressive people on paper had by far the worst judgement of anyone I have ever met. You don't need a bunch of letters beside your name. You don't even need to know all the jargon. That's easy enough to pick up. *What matters most is the idea, the grit to get it done, and the self-confidence to know that every experience in life has value, especially when you are building a business that deals in customers who are just like you.* Whether you had a lemonade stand as a kid, waited tables, or worked at a store in the mall, you can use every scrap of what you know about quality and service from just about anything you have ever turned your hand to. You *are* qualified.

Looking back, I realize that, even though I didn't have the conventional business background or know all the terms, every single one of my jobs has contributed to my strengths as a CEO. One of my earliest experiences in giving the customer what she, or he, wants came from working part-time in a local bridal shop while I was still in high school. I loved helping the brides get ready for their big day and took a lot of satisfaction in listening to what they were looking for and pulling the right dresses. The looks on their faces when they tried on the perfect gown was magical.

One day, in the middle of the week when the store was quiet, two gentleman came in asking if they could try on some of the pageant dresses we carried. It was my first encounter with anyone in the transgender community, and at first I was embarrassed. *What if a bride comes in and gets scared away?* I wondered. It was the early '90s, and they were dressed in unisex clothes, wearing full makeup. To call them an odd sight in the middle of small-town North Carolina would be an understatement, especially back then. But they were as nice as could be, even a little shy about the situation. I reminded myself that they were also customers and that their money was just as good as anyone else's.

"Well, sure!" I said, and grabbed as many of the gowns in the larger sizes as I could.

We had a ball. They spent the next few hours trying on beaded and sequined dress after dress, strutting and vamping in tiaras in front of the full-length mirrors. The afternoon flew by, and they ended up buying two dresses each.

I told the shop owner what happened, and she was delighted.

"Oh my gosh, those are my favorite customers," she said. "They always pay cash and buy the most expensive dresses in the shop!"

Apparently there was a secret community of cross-dressers in the county, and the bridal store was one of their favorite places to shop.

This taught me that it doesn't matter who is buying your product. As long as you treat them with respect, connect with them at the most human level, and do your utmost to give them what they want, they will keep coming back. I learned that customer engagement is so much more than a transaction. It's a relationship built on a desire to help and support each other.

This experience helped me when, as my first marriage ended, I started selling furniture to support myself and my son, Kade. I was one of the top sellers on the floor and quickly earned a spot in the store's "million-dollar club." I decorated the homes of all kinds of wealthy and high-profile people, each with very different tastes and needs. I made a point of getting to know each of my clients and analyzing the full scope of their lifestyles and preferences, and got really quick at reading people from all walks of life. This gave me an understanding of the importance of customization.

When I married Will, and before I had Bella, I opened up a day spa. Bored with being a stay-at-home mom, I told my husband that before I left Florida I was in the process of opening a day spa, so he gave me a $20,000 loan to help me set one up in Lexington—the Temple Spa. Rent was cheap in Lexington, so I found an attractive space and hired massage therapists, a nail technician, and bought all the necessary equipment. In the front of the store I sold a selection of jewelry I'd sourced from a local wholesale place. After a while, the jewelry sold better than the services, so I started stocking dresses and handbags.

It turns out I had an eye, and the shop got so popular I had to move to a bigger location. Soon it was more of a full boutique than a spa. I learned how to spin the latest trends, making a pair of gaucho pants feel just right on a sixty-five-year-old real estate agent or a thirtysomething mom who wanted to be a trendsetter at her club. It was a question of mixing and matching individually appropriate tops and accessories, something I had done in middle and high school when I bought thrift-store items, mixed them with one or two high-quality basics my grandmother bought for me at the mall, and made them look cutting edge and brand new.

I also discovered the importance of pricing something just right. ***No matter how much people love what you are selling, there is only so much they are willing to pay for something that is not a necessity.*** What a customer snaps up at twenty-nine dollars will not budge at thirty-nine. You can get away with selling a little black dress, which can be worn multiple times, for sixty-nine dollars. But a sundress, which is just something fun to wear once in a while, has to sell for less.

The store was profitable, but it was a one-woman show. I couldn't leave it in somebody else's hands because no one treats your business the way you do. This wasn't the career for me because I'm a restless soul who needs limitless possibility and I didn't like feeling hemmed in. Having a brick-and-mortar store married me to that location, and I could only grow so much. Meanwhile, I had just given birth to Eva Bella, or "Evil Bella," as we lovingly call her. Bella was a difficult baby, a screamer, and never slept for more than fifteen minutes at a time. I couldn't leave her at home, and I couldn't have a wailing child in a spa while people were trying to get a massage. ***It takes grit to know when to put yourself and your family first. Prioritizing is another form of being scrappy.*** On top of that, I was bored. My ADHD brain needed to move on. I still had enough inventory and equipment that I could liquidate, to pay back Will for the loan. (I never wanted to owe anybody, not even my husband.)

I almost burned out on being a business owner from that experience. But it turned out to be another gift, because it helped me to create the model and parameters for Lolly Wolly Doodle. I didn't want to keep a lot of inventory or be tied to a specific location, where anything from a rainy day to a holiday could dampen sales. I wanted to work from home, after the kids were in bed. And I was determined that I wasn't going to owe anything to anyone—not a relative, not a spouse, not a bank. At any given time I wanted to be able to get up in the morning, ship out the last few dresses, and shut down that computer for good. I did not want to be beholden to anybody. I had to have the freedom to walk away.

The School of Life

You can learn by doing, and you can learn by observing. ***The school of life has many teachers, and they can be right under your nose.*** My family fed my entrepreneurial appetite and informed my approach as a business owner. My father and brothers all chose to work for themselves. I became scrappy by watching my daddy struggle.

He ran his own brick mason business, which meant that when he injured his back there was no more family income. If he hadn't been frugal his whole life, and if both sets of my grandparents hadn't been able to scrape together enough cash and get us caught up on the mortgage, we could have lost our home. Daddy taught us that if we wanted something, we had to work for it, and we each took odd jobs from the time we were in our teens. When my brothers Donnie and Patrick wanted to go to the beach one summer and there was no money to pay for a motel room, Daddy encouraged them to pick and sell wild blackberries on a relative's farm. They sold mountains of the fruit and were covered in scratches, but it was the best Myrtle Beach vacation they ever had, because they earned it.

Even Pappaw imprinted something on me that you just don't learn in business school. Though he never learned to read or write, he was a brilliant man. He managed a veneer plant, which gave him a modest income, and he was a country loan shark on the side. When I visited on weekends, I used to watch him dole out bills to the neighbors, who came back week after week, paying the interest and asking for more. One day, he took me aside and said:

"Littl'un, you know what? If they just didn't spend money for one week, they wouldn't be back."

Donnie and his many careers—car detailer, stripper bar DJ, and professional hunter—also inspired me. Donnie bought a piece of land in South Carolina that was overrun with wild hogs. He loves to hunt, and the state government there has a program that encourages people to cull the animals, so he started a guided hog-hunting business he jokingly calls "HAWGS-R-US." It earns him a nice living, not that he needs much to be comfortable. He lives in a double-wide trailer and drives the same beat-up ole pickup truck. But he has no debt, no mortgage to pay, and more than enough cash to do what he loves most, like raise chickens, treasure-hunt in a local junk yard, and shoot things. That's what success looks like to him.

My point is that every single scrap of my life had gotten me much further along the entrepreneurial path than any MBA could have. There I was, doing my thing in what I believed to be the relative obscurity of North Carolina's hill country, and somehow I'd become a case study whose social media stats were being quoted at tech conferences across the globe.

But then I hit a ceiling. I was overwhelmed and exhausted, unable to see a better, smarter, and faster way until Shana came along a month later. Through her charm and persistence, I found myself face-to-face with a one-woman powerhouse and realized that this was someone who could teach me a thing or two. There is a difference between blissful ignorance and willful ignorance. ***Just as it is important not to get too caught up in expertise or the textbook way of doing things when you are in the start-up phase of a business and creating something new, it's essential to educate yourself if you ever hope to grow.*** Many first-time entrepreneurs make the mistake of sticking to their initial formula for success and fail to adjust as the business evolves and conditions change. If I'd done that, I'd still be running my little store on Main Street. I realized there were huge gaps in my knowledge that I needed to fill if Lolly Wolly Doodle was ever going to become a real company. That meeting with Shana made me aware that there might be better and faster ways of doing things and that the potential was far beyond anything I could have imagined.

Google Queen

I am the queen of Googling. ***These days, once you are made aware of what you don't know, there's no excuse to stay uninformed.*** So I looked up all of those terms Shana threw at me when we met in New York. I familiarized myself with all the studies she referenced on social media and e-commerce. I researched what a venture capitalist does and got comfortable with the idea of bringing on Shana as a long-term investor. In exchange for the $100,000 note, I gave her a 10 percent stake, but her investment would not be realized unless I raised more funds or sold the company at some point in the future. It would be worth every penny for all of the guidance she has given me.

We talked every couple of days. Shana also connected me with other mentors and colleagues who have taught me to be the business leader I am today. And not a moment too soon. I had been hiring more and more people, and on September 1, just a couple of months after meeting with Shana, I signed our first commercial lease. We'd already exceeded a $1 million run rate, meaning that, based on those few months' performance, our revenues would be far north of that amount. With a tiny overhead and more than enough cash in the bank to fund our expansion ourselves, we didn't need a bank loan. The rent was ridiculously low, on the property that, like many warehouses and factories in the area, was practically a ruin. It had been years since the location had occupants unless you count the bats that had infested half the building. (The manufacturing took place in the other half.) This 4,000–square foot former tire factory, tucked away on one of the back roads of Davidson County, made it official. Lolly Wolly Doodle was a real live business, with real live employees beyond a few church ladies and aunts, and an actual headquarters outside of our garage.

By then I'd hired about a dozen workers. But I had to staff up in every department: sales, customer service, shipping, cutting, sewing, and IT. I'd been trying to do it all myself for too long. Shana wanted me to find some seasoned managers and executives in e-commerce. I'd already been back to New York a couple more times to meet with potential engineers and executives, but nobody clicked until I met another woman who would change my life: Lizzy Johnson.

Soul Sister

"I've got someone I want you to meet," Shana told me excitedly over the phone one day in October 2011. "You'll die when you hear how much she makes, but I want you to think about what she can do for you."

Lizzy was one of those whip-smart tech executives who combines the passion of an entrepreneur with the experience and know-how to dive into any business and fix what is broken. She jumped into start-ups and acted as a kind of cofounder, balancing out weaknesses with her own strengths, which were many. She'd lived a number of past lives, from rocker chick with her own indie band in Portland to crusader against the trade of illegal wildlife. She'd been at the heart of the first Internet boom in 2000, helping to launch a job-searching site, and then developing a photography app way before its time.

The run at her last major start-up made her a star in the tech world, but by the time Shana met her, at a kid's birthday party, she was done with start-ups and ready to live a quiet life somewhere with her husband and two young children. Then Shana showed her a write-up of Lolly Wolly Doodle and changed her mind. It was just the kind of bootstraps, American Dream story she'd been searching for.

Of course, I knew none of this when we met for the first time at our factory. Lizzy showed up in jeans and a baseball cap, and I'm not even sure if she took the time to run a comb through her hair that morning. Before she arrived, I told my staff to clean up the office and be on their best behavior. We still laugh about that. People in technology companies tend to be casual, and she was at the far end of the laid-back spectrum. I liked her immediately.

"You're such a badass!" she told me when she toured the factory, which was humming with the sound of industrial sewing machines and full to bursting with bolts of fabric, boxes of blanks, accessories and trims. Made in the USA had become such a thing of the past that anyone who came to our little corner of the world was amazed. "You're the girl next door building the American Dream!"

Finally, I had my sidekick. On one level, Lizzy and I could not have been more different. I was the cheerleader and pageant queen, and she was the earthy, crunchy granola girl who studied at an Ivy League school and gave liftoff to some of the most important Internet start-ups of this century. She was a technology geek who spoke a language I couldn't understand. And yet it seemed like we were meant to be friends and partners. Our sense of humor was identical. She was a cutup, just like me. We were exactly the same age. Lizzy grew up in St. Louis, so she shared my Middle American roots, and she attended the University of North Carolina, a stone's throw from Appalachia State, where I studied for a spell.

I paid myself less than half what I was paying her as chief operating officer, but it was well worth it. Before Lizzy came along, all we had beyond Facebook was a tiny plug-in website that no one bought from or browsed. She helped me build up the e-commerce side of the business from scratch, increasing our revenue tenfold within a year. She hired engineers, talking and liaising with them to help us build a website that could bring in customer traffic and systems that would streamline customer service and sales. She walked me through the whole process, from marketing, branding, production, and shipping, identifying inefficiencies and helping us build an infrastructure that could actually support our one-of-a-kind business model. She helped me to believe in and understand what e-commerce actually was and what it could be outside of Facebook.

Most of all, Lizzy taught me how to be a leader. When I started Lolly Wolly Doodle, it was very much a family operation. My mother was no longer working then, but I'd since hired my brother Patrick as well as a few cousins and a couple of nieces. Even my husband and my father had part-time jobs at the Doodle. I didn't think of myself as a boss and had no sense of hierarchy. I was always pitching in on the factory floor, sewing pieces or doing whatever was necessary to get product out the door. That was all fine. It set an example. But what Lizzy made me realize was that I could not openly vent or complain in front of my workers, because it undermined my department heads. ***The chain of command could not be broken. I had to play my position as CEO and trust my management team. It was my responsibility to consult with them and handle issues quietly and discretely if I disagreed with how things were being done. I was not one of the girls.*** My managers had to be out there on the front lines while I had to focus on what I was best at—creating new lines, figuring out ways to reach more customers, continuously breaking the "Facebook code," interacting with customers, and being the face of the brand.

It took some reinforcement for that message to sink in. If someone did something to annoy me, I was quick to vent in an e-mail or rant in a Facebook post. I was a little too "in the moment." No one wanted to be on the receiving end of one of my angry memos at the end of a busy day, because it would ruin the rest of their night. Lizzy was the one person who could give it to me straight and tell me when I was out of line. She reminded me that a leader needs to have a filter. ***And she taught me a communication trick that I used to this day: the love sandwich. It's basically a vehicle for delivering not-so-positive feedback in the nicest possible way.***

"I so appreciate your hard work over this past year, but lately I've noticed you don't seem to be as passionate about your work. What can we do together to fix that?" (The "but" is the meat in the middle.)

God put Shana and Lizzy on my path at that juncture in my life for a reason. They pulled me out of survival mode and into growth mode. Without them, Lolly Wolly Doodle wouldn't be the company it is today. Without them, I wouldn't be the woman I am today. He understood that I simply couldn't continue to carry the load by myself. Being a company founder is a lonely business. Yes, I had an amazing team to support me (more about them later). But sometimes you need a peer—someone to bounce ideas off of, call you on your BS, and not yes you to death simply because you are their employer. ***You always need someone to raise the bar for you and make you better.*** Even though Lizzy was on our payroll, she was always an equal. In fact, she was the sister I never had. This was gonna be fun!

AH-HA'S

- You don't have to be an expert. It may even be better if you are not. Many successful entrepreneurs get their start by not knowing the limits. Understanding how things are supposed to be done can throw up false barriers and curb the imagination.
- Learn and observe from the school of life. Anyone can be a teacher.
- What matters most is the idea, the grit to get it done, and the self-confidence to know that every experience has value, especially when you are building a business that deals in customers who are just like you.
- It doesn't matter who is buying your product. As long as you treat them with respect, connect with them at the most human level, and do your utmost to give them what they want, they will keep coming back.
- No matter how much people love what you are selling, there is only so much they are willing to pay for something that is not a necessity.
- You can learn by doing, and you can learn by observing. The school of life has many teachers, and they can be right under your nose.
- Connections, even if it's a friend of a friend of a friend, are key. You'd be surprised who you can find when you ask around.
- Understand the difference between blissful ignorance

and willful ignorance. Just as it is important not to get too caught up in expertise or the textbook way of doing things when you are in the start-up phase of a business and creating something new, it's also essential to educate yourself if you ever hope to grow.

- In the age of Google, once you are made aware of what you don't know, there's no excuse to stay uniformed.
- Deliver criticism with the love sandwich. "I appreciate you but … how can we improve?" It's basically a vehicle for delivering not-so-positive feedback in the nicest possible way.
- You always need someone to raise the bar for you and make you better.

Three

Hire the Person, Not the Resume

Grit is good for you. A little hard work never hurt anybody.

–JERRY TYSINGER, A.K.A. POPS

I was sitting in our Leonard Road factory, looking at fabric swatches and thinking about the next batch of designs, when I heard a faint knocking on our door. As I opened it, a petite elderly woman was standing there, looking neat as a pin in her Sunday best.

"I don't know what y'all are doing in there, but are you hiring?" she asked.

Miss Daisy was seventy-two years old. She had never worked as a seamstress before, with little experience cutting or sewing. But she was desperate for work. Her husband had a heart condition, and they could no longer afford his medication, which wasn't covered by Medicare.

"We've lost everything, and I just need a job really bad," she told me, through tears. "I need to earn some money to keep him alive."

My heart melted. Of course I hired her. How could I not?

It meant we had to take the time to train her, but I needed as many hands as I could get, and something told me someone like Miss Daisy would be so grateful for the work that she'd give it all she had (she did). If it didn't work out on the sewing station, I could try her on cutting. If it didn't work out on cutting, I could set her up making hair bows. We'd find her something, because there sure was plenty to do. As it happens, she became one of our best cutters.

As soon as we moved out of the garage, a stream of people came knocking, literally knocking, on our door. This was shortly after I met Shana and before I hired Lizzy, when our insane pace of growth just seemed to happen all by itself. I'm not even sure how they found us. Our factory, which back then was located along a small access road off the North Carolina Highway, didn't have signage, unless you count a piece of paper we stuck on the entrance to the building after being there for a couple of months. And yet somehow word had spread. The local economy had been so depressed for so long, with the official unemployment rate hovering around 14 percent in 2010, that we were the only sign of life for miles. When I was a little girl, Lexington was a hub for textile manufacturing, both for upholstery and clothing, but over the past couple of decades those jobs had disappeared overseas, mostly to China. The recession only made things worse. All that was left of our town was antique shops and dozens of decaying red brick factories. If anything, our biggest industry was pit barbecue.

One by one, more people found their way to our door, asking for work. They told me the same story. "I've lost my house. I've lost my car. I'll do anything, please just give me chance." I hired them all. It finally got to the point where my staff wouldn't allow me to answer the door anymore.

Many of the women, and a few men, I hired would not even be considered by other businesses. Some had skills that did not appear to be the slightest bit relevant. Laura, for example, my original computer engineer who was responsible for the entire technical infrastructure of the company, was a forklift driver. She taught herself how to be an HTML coder so that she could earn some extra money to raise her grandchild. Talk about grit!

Others who had worked in clothing manufacturing had been out of work for so long their experience would have been written off as obsolete. I hired nurses, schoolteachers, store sales assistants, and stay-at-home moms. Some were fresh out of school. Several weren't that much younger than Miss Daisy, and only a handful knew how to operate industrial sewing machines.

But I believe in listening to my gut and taking a chance on people who may not look perfect on paper. It's about the person, not the resume. Besides, there's more than one way to size up a job candidate. Use your imagination to see what job experience might be an asset, even if it isn't a straight line from one role to the next. *Every piece of information someone picks up along the way can have value.*

When I hire I look for passion, the desire to learn, and a love for the product. Lord knows, if I judged strictly on qualifications, I wouldn't have given myself a chance. I had nothing but respect for these mothers and grandmothers who were willing to put themselves out there and do anything to put food on the table for their families. These women, and men, had true grit. They were folks just like me, willing to use every scrap they had to make their lives better. When they walked up to our building they were nervous. Trying something new, putting yourself out there after constant disappointment is scary. But they instinctively hit that reset button. ***They understood that if you don't take that leap, you'll never know if you've got wings.***

It's well worth putting people to the test. Instead of assuming what someone can't do, try them out on something to see whether they have an aptitude. Shortly after we moved out of our garage, I hired Alison Tysinger, a distant cousin, to help my mother out with invoicing. She'd graduated with a teaching degree and was waiting on a job, so she worked for us part-time to earn a little extra cash. Pretty soon she left us for her dream assignment teaching middle school. She came running back to us three months later. I put her on invoicing again, but on a whim I asked her to fill in for a member of our tech team, which was looking into system glitches. She rocked it. By the end of the day she had the problem solved. Now she is on our tech team full-time, checking for bugs on all of our new releases, anticipating different scenarios to make sure all of our rollouts go smoothly. Her role is critical, but if we hadn't tried her out, I'd have missed a golden opportunity.

Traditionally, companies look at education and knowledge, but when you are a rural manufacturing business starting from scratch, you don't always have that luxury. ***Forget headhunters, job boards, and LinkedIn. We had to find people wherever we could, in and around the commu-***

nity, at our local Walmart, churches, medical offices, schools, and hospitals. While I was out running errands, I'd observe people, watching how they interacted with others and focused on their tasks, whether it was refilling my diet soda at a restaurant or checking me out at the supermarket. If they seemed cheerful and diligent, I'd strike up a conversation and find out more about them. That's how I hired Katie Decker, who was the owner of a local children's gym. She was so chipper and bright, I made her a part of our social media and sales team.

Lolly 101

The fact was that an employee with the perfect, ready-made skill set to walk in to our factory and know exactly what to do simply did not exist, because what we were doing had never been done before. *That's why we had to develop a kind of in-house apprenticeship.* In return, our staff had to be fast on their feet and willing to try new things on an almost weekly basis. We had developed a manufacturing process and supply chain that fed off the cues our customers were giving us on social media. We were developing a kind of mass customization in real time. Each dress was essentially made to order.

Because it was pretty obvious which of our designs were hits and which were misses based on the reactions in the Facebook newsfeeds, we could tailor our designs accordingly. If a particular dress, say an A-line seersucker, sold well one day, I would post a similar one the next. This meant I didn't have to keep reinventing the patterns so much as change out the fabric or add a ruffle here or a trim there. If people were going crazy for it, I could go deep into that style or those colors. And if it didn't, forget it. I didn't make it again. We would fill whatever orders we got and move onto something else. As a result, we never got bogged down with inventory. We could keep our overheads much lower than most other clothing manufacturers and retailers, so that our consumer could get something that was both high quality and affordable. But it also meant that our workers had to be nimble.

They had to be willing to learn a new pattern, or adapt to any variations on our design pods, quickly. To minimize the learning curve, we would have a dozen people cutting fabric according to order tickets. At the sewing stations, those orders would be bundled according to the type of sewing required. The fewer hands or machines that touched the garment, the better and faster, for a flawless personalized product that was out the door in a matter of days.

As Tom Foster, a business writer who later profiled us in *Inc.* put it, "If traditional garment manufacturing is a pretty straightforward assembly-line affair, the seamstresses at Lolly work more like short-order cooks in a diner where the menu changes daily." That's exactly what it was like.

We expanded so rapidly that we made a few mistakes, and my hiring philosophy has had to evolve as we've grown. But the defining qualities of who makes the Doodle cut remain the same:

- **If you can't find Mr. or Mrs. Right, settle for Mr. or Mrs. Right Now.** When sizing up potential employees,

I rely on my gut to tell me if they are motivated and committed. Nonverbal cues like eye contact, facial expressions, and posture tell me whether they are enthusiastic and sincere, which is all I ask. Attitude is everything. They can always learn and improve on the job. Meanwhile, there's work to be done.

- **Look for cat-like reflexes.** You don't want someone who just sits there and waits to be told what to do. One of my stars, my assistant, Katie (not to be confused with sales Katie), anticipates everyone's needs so perfectly that things get done even before they appear on my radar.

- **Reward the doers and shakers.** These are the people who are willing to shake up their routines and jump in wherever necessary, whether it's in their job description or not. They don't whine and complain about overtime, and they *never* say, "That's not what I was hired for."

- **Look for a genuine interest in what you are doing.** Many on our team bought Lolly Wolly Doodle clothes for their children long before they were employees. That wasn't a requirement, but the fact that they were moms and appreciated the product was definitely a plus, because it meant they could identify with our customers. Others just loved the idea that we were bringing jobs back to Lexington and making something tangible and real in our factory. They connected with that and wanted to be part of the story.

- **Seek out overachievers who are goal oriented.** I am one of these people who goes over the top in everything I am doing. I can't just pick up a book and start reading it, because I will stay up all night until it's finished. Ever since I was a little girl, I've been highly competitive. I don't just love a challenge; I have to win. Our best employees are never satisfied with good enough. They want every romper, baby bubble, and A-line dress they stitch to be a best seller.

The Standouts

Amy Vestal was all of the above. She had the LWD DNA.

An obstetrics nurse at our local hospital and my next-door neighbor, Amy's daughter Reese and Eva Bella were born six months apart, and the girls used to play together all the time. Like a lot of my earliest and best hires, Amy was a customer before she joined Lolly Wolly Doodle. In fact, she was into our clothes before the Doodle could have even been considered a company. She loved the innocence of our matchy Southern styles and bought several outfits for Reese, a breathtakingly beautiful child who was one of our models for many years.

Amy, who made hair bows on the side, became my helper and traveling buddy when I went on the road to sell Lolly Wolly Doodle clothes at local festivals and Junior League shows. At first I asked her if she'd make a few bows to match the outfits I was sewing, then she'd stop by the garage after a shift at the hospital, pitch in, and chat. She was the type who likes to keep busy, and she picked up on things quickly, so I knew she'd be the perfect companion for those long trips to Alabama, Kentucky, South Carolina, Tennessee, and Georgia, where most of those charity league events were held.

It was a grind. At first, I did the regional festivals. I knew they were good places to sell stuff without much overhead because Lexington held its own, very profitable, Barbecue Festival every year. Did I mention I once reigned as Barbecue Festival Queen? (Okay, fine. Miss Piggy.) I Googled and found out where and when all the towns within a few hours' drive were having festivals, loaded up a trailer with a monogram sewing machine, inventory, and racks, and set out at the crack of dawn to set up my stall. But it was worth it, because the fee was only about $100, and I could sell between $2,000 and $5,000 worth of dresses by the end of a long day, with no invoicing or shipping to deal with afterward. It was also a great way to get to know our customers face-to-face.

The problem was, these festivals took place rain or shine. They were outdoors under a tent, usually in the middle of a street or field somewhere, at least half a mile from the nearest parking lot. If it was raining, we'd have to trudge through the mud, lifting boxes of clothes, our machine, and our generator. We each kept a pair of rain boots in the car just in case. By the time the festival kicked off at 8 a.m., we were exhausted.

A lady I met at one of these events told me about the Junior League shows. In the South, there are different women's organizations that get together and raise funds for charities, and in the months leading up to back to school and Christmas they rent out these huge halls for shows where people can sell their wares. You have to book a spot months in advance, but once you've set up your booth you don't have to dismantle until the event closes, usually by the end of the weekend. Best of all, you can typically sell $15,000 to $25,000 worth of inventory over those two to four days.

Amy made it all seem less like work than an outing with one of my best girlfriends. Those hours-long drives in my Montero, crossing so many county and state lines, flew by as we joked and laughed and talked about our families. It was like she could read my mind. She'd dress the mannequins, set up the cash registers, hang pictures, haul boxes, set up her display rack with bows, put up the grid walls, and generally help me create the rest of the Lolly Wolly Doodle space exactly the way I wanted. Like me, she was a perfectionist with an eye for detail. And she didn't mind all that carrying and lifting one bit.

She was great with the customers too. It got so crazy that I actually had to rent out two stalls to accommodate all the traffic flow around our booth, which was causing a ruckus and upsetting the other vendors. And the crowds would fight over our items. If there was only one size in a garment laid out on the display table, it wasn't uncommon for two ladies to grab it at the same time and start pulling, like a mini tug-o-war.

"Now there's no need to argue," Amy would tell them in that soothing bedside voice of hers. "It's not like it's the last plate of food!"

We typically didn't keep extra inventory. When the last size was gone, it was gone. But Amy would take special orders that we would fulfill as soon we got back home.

Amy did all of this in her time off, partly to make a little spare cash but mostly out of a passion for what I was doing. On the side, in addition to making her hair bows and doing the Junior League shows with me, she'd been helping me to design products, photograph them, and get them listed for sale on Facebook. If I had to run out and take care of something, I could download everything that needed to be done to her and trust that she knew it cold.

She had an incredible memory for detail. Amy would be gone a week doing long shifts at the hospital, then come back and know everything about what was going on in our business, top to bottom, back to front. She could answer any questions about our products as if she had never walked away. She knew all the SKUs, and we had hundreds of them. If someone pulled out a dress, she'd remember all the other iterations of the design and which pieces matched. It was like she was in my head, able to execute my vision with barely a word spoken.

When business started exploding, I begged her to join us full-time. She was my sanity. The problem was, she already had a successful career. Around the time we moved into our first factory space she had completed her Bachelor of Science degree in nursing, which would have led to more responsibility and a higher salary. ***But if you want something badly enough, ask for it.*** If only she'd slip into a role as my right hand, it would take such a huge burden off my shoulders.

"Girlfriend, is there any way I can convince you to leave your job as a nurse and come to the Doodle full-time?" I asked her. "I'll make it worth your while."

Amy thought long and hard about it, then she made the leap. She loved nursing. But she enjoyed being creative even more. From the age of fifteen she helped out a lady in a gift basket shop, creating balloon sculptures and assembling all the items to go in each basket. Before long she was running the place, doing the books, handling sales, ordering supplies. . . . Ever since then she wanted to do something entrepreneurial but never imagined it would be possible. The fact that I would pay her more than her salary as a nurse sweetened the pot. It was one of the best investments I ever made.

Amy started out listing sales on Facebook, which in the beginning was no small task. We would list as quickly as Amy could go into the warehouse, count the product, and figure out which items to sell, posting throughout the day–and night. As the system developed, we were able to post items automatically and then go home to watch the Facebook feeds fill up with comments and orders. Amy would help me analyze those customer responses to figure out the winners.

Back then we would design two or three items, make the patterns, and sell them online that day. But we held back the special posts for the evening–either things our customers hadn't seen before or a best seller in a new fabric that we had just gotten in. People went crazy for these items, which encouraged a lot of sales. That's one of the ways we built up our Facebook likes. So Amy's role was critical, not to mention time consuming.

From sales, Amy switched to design and fabric sourcing. Anything I needed her to do, she would just jump in and learn. Within a year I promoted her to vice president of sales and design. Today she's in charge of all product development and new product releases. She also puts in the occasional shift at the hospital to keep up her nursing qualifications, which is good for us, because some of our best customers and baby models have come straight from Amy's maternity ward, including her fellow nurses.

Another standout was my niece Jordan. Like I said, this is a family business. When I first started, it was my family who pitched in to help, and most ended up staying, growing with the business alongside me. But, make no mistake, they earn their paychecks.

Jordan, who is my middle brother Patrick's oldest daughter, was a high school math teacher. During her summer breaks she would come and do shows with us. As we expanded, I asked her to come and help out full time in the warehouse, overseeing all fulfillment operations. She was such a fast learner that, after a couple of years, she ended up working with our engineering team in New York, where she learned technology product development and helped to design our ERP system.

ERP, short for enterprise resource planning, is software that allows businesses to use a system of integrated management software that can automate all kinds of back-office functions. The customer doesn't see how this works directly, but she experiences it through the efficient way we process her order, from the fabrics and customization details she chooses on a garment to the speed of delivery onto her doorstep, when the product arrives exactly according to her specifications and expectations. Our system was especially complex, because it enabled our customers to talk to our sales system, which had to be seamless and lightning quick. Jordan understood the language of IT, but she also knew our customer service and sales needs, so she became the critical link between the engineering and sales team—a skill set that is one of the most highly sought after among e-commerce companies around the world. That's quite a change from teaching freshman algebra!

Lolly, Jordan's sister and our company's namesake, joined us fresh out of high school to make bows. She soon moved into the social media sales side, listing on Instagram and Facebook. She's involved in developing ads, sending out e-mails, and every aspect of marketing. It comes naturally to her. These functions tend to be separate in traditional companies, but at the Doodle they are all intertwined. Everyone works side by side in the same room. Millennials grew up with this technology, so they adapt quickly to any changes and are used to multitasking. If they had just one specific role, a job that never changed, they'd soon get bored. And the fact is that all of these activities are closely connected. The social sales and marketing teams need to talk to each other to respond quickly to trends and keep the message consistent.

Doodle Blossoms

One of my greatest joys as a business owner is getting to see how, given the chance, people can blossom. So many on the Doodle team have risen in ways they never would have dreamed possible. I especially love it when they surprise me.

When Brittany Weaver tottered into our bat-infested warehouse dressed in Daisy Dukes and stiletto heels, I had no intention of hiring her and only did so because my son,

Kade, begged me to. Fresh out of high school, with a great little body and a precious face, she looked like she stepped right off the pages of a Frederick's of Hollywood catalogue—not your typical small-town Lexington look. She had no qualifications or experience, but I gave her a shot at listing sales. Turns out she had a real eye for fashion, and she's since grown into our head of merchandizing. She's hardworking and determined, with a raw honesty that takes my breath away. One day she looked straight at me and declared, "I'm gonna work so hard that I'll be wearing Gucci and driving a Mercedes." I believed her.

Running a company is like cultivating a garden. The potential for your employees' talents to flower was inside them all along—they just needed the right conditions and care. It just goes to show that when you give someone your trust and faith, miracles can happen.

Jackie and Erica, who head up my design team, exceeded their own expectations. They both started out as seamstresses, but they had the eye and the creativity to do so much more.

Jackie, a sixty-two-year-old great-grandmother, joined us early on, in April 2011. It's been especially gratifying to give hope to an older generation of seamstresses who believed they were all out of chances. When we started growing, I promised Daddy I'd do everything I could to bring back jobs to our town and give the textile industry life again. But it went both ways. These women gave back to us tenfold with their dedication and loyalty.

Jackie has been in the textile industry since the early '70s, and of course those jobs had long since been contracted overseas. She tried her hand at her own business, making medical uniforms, but shuttered it in 2010 when the economy took a turn.

"I thought, nobody is going to hire me at my age," she later told me.

She'd been out of work a week and was about to venture, reluctantly, into retail, when fate stepped in. Feeling that her life was at a standstill, Jackie went out for a coffee one morning and came across a copy of the *Davidson Reporter*, a local newspaper insert she almost always threw away. It was a pretty day, and something told her to sit outside on the porch and read it. There happened to be a story about Lolly Wolly Doodle and the fact that we were looking for seamstresses. Jackie figured, "Why not?" Once again, this wasn't random. God was working his miracles again. Ah-ha!

I needed someone just like Jackie, who was eminently qualified. For fifteen years she had made women's nightwear for Sears and JCPenney. It took her no time to get up to speed with the newest industrial sewing machine, and she ended up training dozens of our other sewers. She had the patience and personality that put others at ease.

One of her trainees was Erica, a shy stay-at-home mom who used to sew her children's clothes so they would have something wholesome to wear—like me. Erica had also been a faithful Lolly Wolly Doodle customer, so when she was filling out job applications at the mall and a woman at Chick-fil-A mentioned we were hiring, she drove straight here. I hired her that day.

She didn't think she'd be asked back the next day. The industrial machines were too quick for her, and she botched a few things. But who hasn't had a bad first day? ***I believe in giving people the time and space to get up to speed,*** and she sure did. Of course it depends on the nature of your business and the level of technical expertise required, but sometimes it is better to hire underqualified people if they are hungry and eager. Within eight months Erica was the sewing department supervisor. Soon after that she started sourcing fabrics for us.

Today she works under Jackie in our design department, coming up with ideas for new looks and fabrics we design in house, and testing them out by running up samples. Together, they are like my creative right arm, constantly bringing me new ideas, many of which have been huge hits with our customers. But when you point out to Erica the fact that she is now a lead designer for a national ladies' and children's clothing brand, she blushes. Jackie just chuckles and smiles.

Steel Magnolias

A typical human resources manager would blanch at my interview methods. But I have had so much more success trusting my instincts than following the conventional rules, especially when it comes to building up my Lolly Wolly Doodle team. Most companies put job candidates through extensive interviews and a variety of tests. They check references, have the applicant draw up a 30/60/90 plan, and then meet with board members. Depending on the seniority of the position, some of those techniques may apply. But none of these methods really give me what I need to know about the person. We like to ask questions that tell us who the potential employee is and how they react to situations. *Can you dance? Can you iron?* (So relevant.) The answers you get are priceless.

So were some of the characters who ended up on our factory floor, like Sandra Tussey, who we called the "Easter Bunny" because of the high, puffy little ponytail she always wore. We all squealed with laughter when Sandra, who had dentures, broke a front tooth at work and glued it back on (we also called her "Super Glue"). She wasn't the fastest worker we had, but an absolute sweetheart, and she got the job done.

Then there was Peaches, who worked in our applique department and was so much fun to tease. We never did get rid of all the bats that had infested the other side of our first factory location. Apparently there is some statute that forbids killing the critters. You have to bring someone in to catch and release, and somehow the bats would always find their way back again. They hung out in the back, but as we grew we had to move the workstations closer and closer to that rear wall. And there was a particular door we were terrified to open, because each time a startled bat or three would fly into our faces.

Peaches was especially nervous about anything creepy crawly. So one Halloween Adam, who worked in customer service, tied a fake bat to a string and dropped it down whenever someone from the floor walked through, which they invariably would, because the only way they could get to the restroom was to walk through customer service and my office. Peaches was our best victim. When she was done screaming she wrestled Adam to the ground. She had him in an arm lock until he begged for mercy. We only picked at those who could pick back.

Fire on the Mountain

Donna Yates, or Grumpy as we lovingly called her, was a veteran seamstress for the North Carolina furniture and garment industry. She had been unemployed for about two years before she heard there was a job opening from her sister, who'd joined us a month earlier. Over the past twenty-five years, she'd switched from sewing blue jeans and ladies' skirts to the heavier, more industrial work of producing foam and cushions for the furniture industry. She worked at each job until the factory closed down, enduring one disappointment after the other, but always up for whatever opportunity came along until the last factory shipped its jobs to China. (And don't get her started on that topic unless you really want to see what cranky looks like.)

"I never thought I'd see this day again," she told me when she was hired. "I thought it was over. No more made in the USA, but I got fooled."

A sixty-four-year-old grandmother, Grumpy hated being put out to pasture. "You can only clean house and wash clothes so much." Besides, she needed to keep working to cover her disabled husband's medical bills and help out her grown children, who were still struggling after the recession hit. Now she's one of my fastest sewers and operates the serger, a tricky five-thread operation that locks in a seam on a garment to prevent it from fraying. She is also a kind of un-official drill sergeant on the sewing floor.

Value the older generation. They have a work ethic that's getting increasingly rare these days. It doesn't matter if they're not up on the latest technology. They can learn. Anyone can learn if you are patient enough to teach them what they need to know.

Grumpy was old school. If people were getting sloppy and not paying attention, she'd have something to say about it in that deep, raspy chain-smoker's voice of hers. I get it. We all make mistakes. But making the same stupid one over and over again is a sign you don't care enough to get it right, and Grumpy hated seeing this job being taken for granted. She wouldn't mind if you called her a redneck and tough as old boot leather, but it all came from a place of love. She kept her own grandchildren in line with the words, "Fire on the mountain!" That meant their rumps would turn red from a good spanking, and we were always afraid she'd do the same thing to us if we got on her bad side.

On one of her first days at the Doodle I caught some of that temper. It was nothing for me to go out on the floor and sit at one of the machines if it was empty. I sat down behind Donna and asked her, "Are you closing that from the top?"

She was on the serger at the time, and the machine was giving her a fit, so I couldn't have picked a worse time to say something.

"What?!" she said, and turned around with a scowl on her face. Then her eyes got big.

"Oh, I'm so sorry, I didn't know who it was!"

From that day forward she was known as "Grumpy." Even

when a *Good Morning America* camera crew came in, I told them, "You gotta meet Grumpy."

"Im'ma kill you," she said, laughing. Actually she's proud of the nickname. She even wears it on a T-shirt.

We've had all kinds of crazy–funny crazy and scary crazy– and our cast of characters didn't always get along. When the pressure was on to fill orders during peak times, like before Easter or Christmas, scissors would fly and fistfights would break out. Even sweet little ole Miss Daisy lost it one time and threw a pair of shears at one of the other cutters. Usually the eruption was over as soon as it started. People would bless each other out and be done with it. But "Mudd" was the exception.

Volcanic Eruption

Mudd, a fiftysomething biker's moll and the fastest sewer on the floor, could be especially ornery. She was big and burly, and looked like one of the extras on that show *Orange Is the New Black*. I'm not sure where she learned to sew. Prison, perhaps? She didn't share much information about her life, which I gathered had not been easy. But she could stitch together a dress in twelve minutes; it took anyone else twice as long. And her work was precise. I'd never known her to make a mistake.

But it had reached a point where people felt threatened. When she saw the hijinks we were playing in the office, she took Adam aside and said, "I'll let you in on a little secret. Playing a prank on me is a good way to get your ass kicked." And you could tell she meant it.

Mudd had a thing about personal space. If someone accidentally brushed up against her chair or touched her stuff, she exploded with rage. Within a year we had already outgrown our Leonard Road space so it was close quarters, and that meant more than a few eruptions as Mudd either could not or would not adapt to the changing conditions. We were running out of parking spaces on our lot, and she took exception to being asked to park in between the lines.

"I'll park any way I damn well want to."

She finally crossed the line when a woman accidentally pushed her chair into the back of Mudd's and she responded with, "I'm gonna beat your ass!"

The Ice Queen

We saved it all for Jamie Everhart to handle.

Jamie was another neighbor, although until she joined the Doodle team I didn't know her very well. She came to a couple of the sales when we were making dresses out of our garage, and we exchanged a few pleasantries at the occasional children's party in somebody's backyard. But we were just passing acquaintances. I did know that she was the human resource manager at Silver Eagle LLC, which was a regional distributor for Anheuser-Busch. Will and I used to watch her driving past our house early each morning. She always looked so polished and professional.

One morning during a particularly tough week at the Doodle, we waved at Jamie driving up the road as usual, and Will said, "That's who you need. Someone like her."

It was another ah-ha moment. I'd been struggling with HR issues for a while. We grew and hired so fast that the situation was getting unruly. But firing people is one of the hardest things any business leader has to do. ***One of our investors once told me "a good CEO knows how to hire quickly, but a great CEO knows how to fire faster."*** I had a ways to go to meet his definition. I've never really gotten used to the fact that disciplining and getting rid of employees I care about, even family members, goes with the territory of being a boss.

The next day I ran into Jamie with her family at our local Subway and stopped to say hello.

"Let me know if you ever need help with HR," Jamie said. "The company I was working with has just been bought out so I will be thinking about my next steps soon."

My jaw dropped. Again, God's timing is perfect. He had put Jamie on my path right when I needed her most. Her last day at her company was October 31, 2011. On November 4, she started working as our first human resources manager. She must have been shocked by what she walked into. We were a casual bunch—jeans, shorts, yoga pants, and tees—yet she always came into work wearing professional business attire and high heels, with immaculate makeup and her hair perfectly styled. On top of that, she had a baptism by fire. I asked her to let go of Mudd on her very first day.

"But I have to warn you, she's an angry lady and she's not going to take it well."

"No problem. I've got this."

Jamie politely asked Mudd to come into her office and informed her that it would be her last day at Lolly Wolly

Doodle. Mudd cussed, called her a string of nasty names, and then threatened to beat her up. But Jamie wasn't flustered.

"Ma'am, I need to you calm down and walk out of this building peacefully, or I will call the police."

Jamie had handled her share of layoffs at Silver Eagle, but nothing like this. When things turned ugly, she had a security team with her to keep things under control. On this day she had my brother Patrick, the only man on the premises at the time.

Patrick happened to be one of two people Mudd tolerated besides Jackie, who got along with everybody. He felt awful about what was happening but did what he was told and gathered up Mudd's things into a tub. He was supposed to take them out to her car so they'd be ready to go when she was escorted outside, but everything unfolded too quickly. He hadn't made it out the door before Mudd and Jamie came back into the sewing area.

"What the hell are you doing with my stuff? Nobody touches my stuff!" Mudd screamed.

"Mudd, I'm so sorry, I'm just following orders here," Patrick replied.

Eventually, Mudd left, and you could feel the tension in the whole factory ease up. But Patrick felt terrible. A few days later he called to try to make things right between them, but she refused to come to the phone. To this day Patrick insists Mudd had a sweet side, "but you had to dig deep to find it."

Jamie's loving-kindness was a lot closer to the surface. In countless ways, she saved me. Nothing seemed to faze her, so we nicknamed her the "Ice Queen." In fact, she internalized everything and cared deeply about everyone's well-being at the Doodle. She quickly became a part of the family, like the strict but loving aunt who made sure people didn't get too far out of line, for their own sakes.

She kept the government officials at bay when they came to inspect the premises. "Just turn your eye to it, and we will get it fixed," she told them. Then she got us up to code.

Making that leap from a corporate background to our factory, which had the atmosphere of a frat house in the early days, had to have been jarring. But she spotted the potential lawsuits and kept us out of trouble, even if it gave her the reputation of resident party pooper.

Margarita Fridays

Folks at the Doodle were a hardworking bunch. No matter what their position, people were willing to wear different hats, jump in where needed, and put in the hours to make shipping deadlines. I liked to reward their hard work and loyalty and alleviate some of the peak-season tension with a few on-the-job perks. I didn't want people to feel it was just a job. I wanted them to feel like the Doodle was their second home—a place where they could get job satisfaction as well as a few moments of hilarity. ***Why not put some fun into the place where you spend most of your waking hours?***

Most summer Fridays at lunchtime, we'd pick a designated driver, take the seats out of the back of my blue minivan (the Smurf), and load it up with as many ladies as we could for tacos and margaritas at a local Mexican restaurant. You'd be surprised how productive people can be after a three-hour liquid lunch. To make sure everyone felt included, Will would take the few men in the factory out for barbecue and a few rounds of golf in the evenings.

I also bought a popcorn machine and a slushy maker. We were nothing like the Google offices, but I tried. We brought in someone to wash employees' cars. We also brought in a manicurist. So many of these woman worked hard at home as well as the factory, making dinner, cooking, and cleaning for their families when they came off a shift. They didn't have time to go to the nail salon, so we brought it to them. A little pampering never hurt anybody, and the boost to self-esteem had the added benefit of a happier and more productive work-force, although that wasn't my main motivation. As I woman I just knew it would help them to feel good and know how much they were valued. That's also why I hired a masseuse. Once in a while, we would even reward workers with fifteen-minute massages at their workstations—usually after a lot of late shifts.

We went all out for birthdays and holidays. On Hallow-een, everyone would get dressed up, I'd throw a party with food and treats on the factory floor, and we'd give out prizes for best costume. One year, Brittany dressed as a bikini-clad pine tree air freshener that said "Da Freshest," because a creepy guy on the floor used to come up behind her, take a big sniff and tell her she smelled so good she could be an air freshener in his car. (He no longer works at the Doodle.) Alison did a hilarious impersonation of Honey Boo Boo, complete with a ruffled hot pink minidress and a bottle of Mountain Dew. Adam always dresses up as a woman and pulls it off so well. One year he posed for pictures as a racy blonde in a tight black dress, hitchhiking outside the factory. The list of creative costumes goes on. Halloween is my favorite holiday hands down, although Christmas is a big deal at the Doodle too. As soon as December rolls around, we decorate the place, throw a huge feast, and give away gifts cards, toys, even televisions for the workers and their children. And everyone gets a cake for their birthday.

Some even got a special dance in their honor. Somehow we'd found out that Rod Stewart was Jackie's favorite singer, so Adam tracked down a blond spiky wig, dressed up like the pop star, and did a little pretend striptease while serenading her with "If ya want my body. . . ."

When we brought out a cake for the next seamstress who had a birthday, she rolled her chair into the middle of the sewing floor and waited with a big expectant smile on her face. We didn't have a dance number planned, but we sent Adam out anyway.

Jamie had to clamp down on a few of these celebrations. We kept the holiday parties, massages, and manicures. But the X-rated birthday cakes and saucy dances had to go. So did the Margarita Fridays. ***We had to transition to a more grown-up workplace culture, although we did our best to maintain the family atmosphere.*** Of course you need to evolve as your business grows, but never forget who you are.

Weeding the Garden

We also had to get rid of a few bad apples. During the early years, we were in triage mode and needed as many skilled or trainable hands as we could get, but some took advantage. Patrick, who now works as our facilities manager overseeing repairs and equipment maintenance, is a quiet, observant type. He noticed one of the cutters used to come in about half an hour earlier than anyone else, claiming she liked to get there extra early to set up her workstation before her shift started. He thought that was suspicious.

We kept large trash bags for the fabric scraps, which Patrick would take out to the Dumpster at the end of each day. He noticed that this lady was throwing bolts of fabric into the scraps bags and taking them home. We asked to see her car, and there they were. We were the only people who carried those particular prints, so that explained why we were finding several pirated dresses for sale around town. We caught a few people using similar methods to thieve. Another woman claimed she was taking home scraps to make pet toys. Of course, once the thieves were found out, they were fired on the spot. But even that didn't stop some. While my entire family, including Patrick, was away on vacation, the pet toy lady had someone come in to the factory and haul off nine truckloads of scrap fabric!

A good gardener knows when to pull the weeds. If she doesn't, they'll spread and choke out the rest of the flowers. I couldn't tolerate dishonest or disruptive workers who were creating tension and drama in their departments, or slackers who put in minimum effort while others carried the load for them. It wasn't fair to everyone else, who needed to see that there was room to stand out and grow.

Jamie took care of most of the dismissals, but I couldn't always avoid those excruciating face-to-face conversations.

Most of all it pained me to know that losing a job could, for many of our employees, lead to a missed mortgage payment and a lost home. Sometimes that job was all they had, and you know it takes every paycheck to barely survive. The local economy has been improving some, but the unemployment rate still hovers at around 10 percent. One of my hires actually told me that if it wasn't for us, she'd be living in a homeless shelter. ***So when you know the stakes, exercising discipline and firing employees can be nauseating, even if it does go with the territory of being a boss.***

It's especially tough in a small town with few opportunities and a ruthless gossip mill. Some of these people were friends, or friends of friends, or neighbors. In some cases, people had family members working at the factory. The thing about operating in a small town is that everyone is related. It can be great for networking and hiring, but what happens if the family member or friend doesn't work out? What happens if the employee is related to me? It could get extremely awkward.

And when you are running a rural business, laid-off workers don't just disappear, they end up as servers at the local Subway, making my lunch. I guess it's a good thing you can see them making your sandwich through the glass.

AH-HA'S

- Listen to your gut, and take a chance on people who may not look perfect on paper. It's about the person, not the resume.
- Look beyond the resume. Use your imagination to see what job experience might be an asset, even if it isn't a straight line from one role to the next. Every piece of information someone picks up along the way can have value.
- Dare to try something new. Putting yourself out there after constant disappointment is scary. But if you don't take that leap, you'll never know if you've got wings.
- Depending on where you are based, you don't always have the luxury of using traditional hiring methods. Find other sources besides headhunters, job boards, and LinkedIn. We had to find people wherever we could, in and around the community, at our local Walmart, churches, medical offices, schools, and hospitals.
- Be open to on-the-job training. Especially when your business is so innovative, you can't assume people will walk in with exactly the right skill set. That's why we had to develop a kind of in-house apprenticeship.
- If you can't find Mr. or Mrs. Right, settle for Mr. or

Mrs. Right Now. Assign a more experienced worker to mentor them for their first week or two. If it's a relatively low-skilled position, they can always learn and improve on the job.

· Look for cat-like reflexes. You don't want someone who just sits there and waits to be told what to do.

· Seek out doers and shakers. These are the people who are willing to shake up their routines and jump in wherever necessary, whether it's in their job description or not.

· Is there a genuine interest in what you are doing? Passion makes up for plenty.

· Seek out overachievers who are goal oriented.

· Running a company is like cultivating a garden. The potential for their talents to flower has been inside them all along—they just need the right conditions and care.

· Who hasn't had a bad first day? Give people the time and space to get up to speed, and your patience will be rewarded.

· Value the older generation. They have a work ethic that's getting increasingly rare these days. It doesn't matter if they're not up on the latest technology. They can learn. Anyone can learn if you are patient enough to teach them what they need to know.

· But realize when the line has been crossed. A wise man once told me, "A good CEO knows how to hire quickly, but a great CEO knows how to fire faster."

- Reward workers with little on-the-job perks. Why not put some fun into the place where you spend most of your waking hours? But keep it professional, people.
- Firing people is the hardest thing you can do as a boss, but a good gardener knows when to pull the weeds. If she doesn't, they'll spread and choke out the rest of the flowers.

Four

Authenticity Beats Originality

Be yourself. Everyone else is already taken.

–OSCAR WILDE

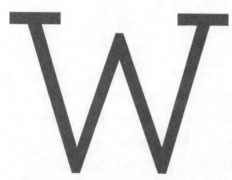hen I first started selling Lolly Wolly Doodle at the local festivals, I met a woman from up North who made belts and headbands for women and children. This lady was a hoot–eccentric, funny, and sharp in her observations as she picked at some of the local characters walking through the festival grounds. She bought something of mine, then asked if I had ever done any of the Junior League shows. At that point I hadn't, but she was quick to fill me in on the awesomeness of these events.

"Let's team up," she suggested. "All I need is one good wall to hang up my belts."

She gave me her contact details, and I e-mailed her when I managed to find a booth at a couple of the pre-Christmas shows a few weeks later. I figured it would be fine, as she wasn't in direct competition with me. Her pretty and unusual accessories could complement my offerings nicely. For the next two years we shared a space, until my sales were so crazy I needed every inch of display wall I could get. When I explained to her it was no longer advantageous to me to share a booth, she grew cool and distant. I was sad, because I thought we had become good friends. Six months later, she was selling a line of children's clothes at the shows and on Zulily.

There will always be copycats. **When you are successful, imitation is a fact of life.** My designs are simple and easy enough to rip off, and dozens of people, even a few former employees, have tried. Whenever we came up with a new design, we'd see a look-alike on the market two weeks later. It's not like you can patent an A-line dress or a romper, and our fabric suppliers were free to sell their prints to anyone. For that reason, I tried not to spend too much time looking over my shoulder. We kept ahead of the ankle biters with better quality, faster delivery, and a loyal community of customers we listened to carefully. We introduced dozens of styles weekly, and we had the technology and creativity to be able to swiftly cater to our moms' changing tastes and needs. Our passion kept us ahead of everyone else.

When you pour your heart and soul into what you do, you don't need to obsess about being the first or the only person to do something. Not everyone is struck by lightning, but you do have your own unique fingerprint. You own a collection of life experiences and impressions that no one else has, and that can bring a flavor and feeling to anything if you put your all into what you are creating, whether that's bubble bath, cupcakes, or kitchen cabinets. The world has billions of people, so they will always need bakers or carpenters or soap makers. You may not be the only one making your product, you may not even be the best, but this is *your* passion. **If this is what you love and need to be doing, you can't help but make it unique in countless subtle ways that add up to something truly special.**

Why try to be a unicorn when you can be a beautiful Clydesdale? Too often people feel embarrassed or insufficient because they didn't reinvent the wheel, to the point where they don't even pursue something. They give up before they start. But what makes people successful is their attitude. I just made cotton dresses. But I worked hard on them. Even a basic A-line pattern, which has been around for years, got the Lolly Wolly Doodle touch with specially chosen fabrics and details. I made sure our clothes had the right price point, the best possible fit, quality, fabric, and everything else, because I realized that, when I gave it my all, people would come.

Some people can't see their own uniqueness. They don't realize what their enjoyment in creating something brings to that product. Don't ever think that just because your cupcakes aren't state of the art, with dozens of trendy gourmet flavors like green tea or lavender, they aren't something that people will desire. They taste better, they are moist, and even if they are plain ole vanilla or chocolate, people will want them because they are made by *you*. (And anyway my favorite cupcake is vanilla with buttercream icing.)

Anyone can be creative. It's all about finding a solution to a problem, then taking action. I didn't plan to do anything special, I just figured something out based on my own needs and desires as the struggling stay-at-home mother of four kids, including two little girls. It just so happened that the world was full of moms who wanted the same for their children. By being determined to live by my own high standards, I tapped into something universal.

In some ways it's better to keep blinders on. The racehorse runs faster when it's not looking to the left or the right. **Don't watch what anybody else is doing too closely. You can be inspired by great work, but never consciously imitate.** At the same time, the worst thing you can do is focus too hard on originality. Never think, *Well, I can't sell these tablecloths because Marjorie already sells table linens and people love hers.* As some of the greatest thinkers throughout history have said, there is no such thing as true originality, because some version of everything under the sun has already been created. Those small details, or simply the way you combine things, provide plenty of originality. But what really brings something newness is the fact that you have infused it with your own soul. So **worry less about being original and more about being authentic**. Or, as Judy Garland says, "Always be a first-rate version of yourself."

The Thirty-Day Rule

Even as a child I was hell-bent on doing me. My mother still laughs about the fact that I kept a journal in middle school, keeping track of everything I wore throughout the school week so that I would never repeat the same outfit twice in thirty days. I didn't have that many clothes to begin with, but I could create different looks through careful mixing, matching, and accessorizing. I had it down to a science.

Truth be told, at that age I *was* guilty of looking over my shoulder. If another kid in school started wearing something identical to what I had, I just wouldn't wear it anymore. When I was seven my father bought me a pair of colored denim pants that had a stripe down one leg. I was so proud of these pants because no one else in school had anything like them, until the next week when my best friend got a pair. Mine went straight to the back of the closet, never to be worn again. I had to be the first and only–a trendsetter.

I managed to be a fashion plate despite the fact that my family had very little cash to spare by picking up separate clothing items dirt cheap at the charity stores. Thanks to Mammaw Betty, I had a trained eye for a true bargain. She taught me what to look for in terms of quality and timeless style. I inspected the stitching, the type of fabric, pattern, and cut. It didn't matter whether it came from the mall or the Goodwill, I could spot something that looked expensive, even if it only cost me two dollars. Then I'd take it home, clean and press it, and mix it in with some store-bought pieces at school the next day. If someone asked me, "Where did you get that?" invariably, I'd say, "Oh, this old thing? Just a little something I picked up."

Mammaw was a huge influence on my sense of style. Neither she nor my mother would let me leave the house without looking immaculate, even when I was a baby. I was their golden-haired princess, and they dressed me up like a little doll.

My mother sewed all my baby clothes, so I always had an assortment of cute little outfits. When I was three years old and went to the hospital to have my tonsils taken out, I wore a pink satin nightgown with a lace collar and a matching housecoat. My hair was curled and tied with a pink satin bow, because I was going to be seen by doctors, nurses, other patients, and their families. Whatever the circumstances, it mattered to my mother and grandmother how I was presented to the world. It was a point of family pride and dignity that their child was dressed up like a little Southern lady. (I still have a picture of that little girl dressed to perfection, kissing my pappaw on the cheek. I keep it on the bookcase behind my desk at the Doodle.)

As a child I had a lot of rules about what to wear and what not to be caught dead in—my very own *Glamour* magazine dos and don'ts. I was so particular, I never wore jeans. I thought women looked hideous in jeans. They were far too sloppy and casual (of course nowadays I live in jeans). I tucked in my shirts neatly, accessorized with a belt. In my earlier years I wore my clean white Keds with ruffled socks, and everything always matched. In high school my hair was always done, teased to the sky and held there with lots of hairspray. I never set foot outside of the house without full makeup and freshly manicured nails. I believed then, as I do now, that every woman must own a strand of pearls. And I never wore white after Labor Day or before Memorial Day. I don't care if Emily Post says it's okay now. It doesn't feel right to me.

These strict Southern style rules must have been ingrained in me by my grandmother. In middle school those weekend visits to Mammaw and Pappaw's house were the highlight of my week. The sun rose and set on Mammaw Betty, a dark-haired beauty who had an old movie-star glamour in her younger years. Without fail, Pappaw would pick me up in his truck and deliver me to their house. Her bedroom was the only room with air conditioning, which was a rarity in those days. She would make me a pallet on the floor, piled high with cushions. It was so comfy. I can still smell the air in that bedroom, scented with the Estée Lauder powder she wore: a crisp smell with hints of rose, lavender, and jasmine.

Those weekends consisted of shopping trips to the mall. Usually I'd just pick up a small accessory or two. But every so often my grandmother would give me a budget of fifty to a hundred dollars, or more on special occasions, and teach me how to spend for value. Not bargains. Value. I learned not to buy something just because it was on sale. She taught me that if it was poor quality and something I'd be unlikely to wear often, the small price tag was a false economy. I could still look at sale racks, but whatever I picked up had to be held to the same standards as something sold at full price. "You don't buy something because it's on sale," she told me. "You buy something because you want it, and if you invest in good clothes you will wear them and get your money back. If it's just a bargain, and that's the only reason you buy it, then it's not a bargain."

Far better to invest in one great quality piece, she told me, than to purchase five tops at Rave. Not that we even entered that store. Mammaw would have passed out in that place! Those shopping trips helped me to build my small collection of staples: crisp white blouses, chambray shirts, cashmere sweaters, perfectly tailored khaki slacks. These were the items I would mix and match with my thrift-store finds. I was a walking poster child for Ralph Lauren and Brooks Brothers, but with my own unique twist on that '80s look of polo shirts, khakis, and bright white Keds that was the high school uniform du jour. I was going for a look that was a balance between edgy and preppy, like something you might see on the most chic Southern women at the country club.

I studied fashion magazines to figure out my own style. I loved any preppy brands that symbolized status and Southern posh. Of course we couldn't afford designer labels. Instead, I would accessorize with a bright scarf and accent an outfit with a print in fresh colors like pink, blue, or green. I almost looked like a sorority girl, although I was never in a sorority. But that's what I was going for: polished, unique, modest yet trendy, and at an affordable price because I had no choice. And I always had to stand out in a crowd. As soon as my look caught on in the rest of the school, I would change it up. As much as I wanted to be a trendsetter, I didn't want to see myself coming.

One of my crowning moments was my prom outfit—a vintage dress with dyed-to-match high-top Converse sneakers. Think *Pretty in Pink* with a Southern belle twist. This was the early '90s before anyone in my corner of North Carolina did vintage or wore high-tops, so I caused a stir and was voted homecoming queen—one of many goals I ticked off my list.

Bright Red Alfa Romeo

Of course, there came a time when I realized I couldn't be first at everything. There is always going to be somebody who has you beat.

My parents were always big planners, a trait I must have inherited from them. They also knew their daughter well. In fourth grade they promised me they'd buy me any car within reason for my sixteenth birthday if I got As, although the occasional B was allowed. I was so motivated I kept my grades up for every report card. I was counting the days until I was old enough to drive. By then they were doing a little better and they'd had a few years to save for it. Getting a car is a rite of passage in these parts, and, besides, Donnie and Patrick weren't planning on giving me rides forever.

Most kids in Lexington drove American cars, so as usual I had to be different. It just so happened that my mother's friend and colleague, a guidance counselor at the high school where she worked, decided to sell her cherry red, mint-condition Alpha Romeo convertible for a great price. It was an older model—Mom and Daddy couldn't afford something brand new—but it looked chic and vintage. I knew I would turn heads as I cruised down Main Street with the top down, my long blond hair flying in the wind, the radio playing something by Bon Jovi or Madonna, which was how most teenagers socialized after school and on weekends in Lexington.

When I got my car I was so proud, until I saw a girl around town driving the exact same model and color. And, gasp, she was also blonde. People would get confused and think she was me. To make matters worse, her high school also crowned her homecoming queen and we had to share the spot in our local paper. Somehow we'd never met before, because she went to another high school. Her name was Amy Davis, and I hated her on sight.

Then we met up again in college. I had zero interest in getting to know this girl, my nemesis, but we ended up sitting next to each other in a class and I couldn't help myself. As soon as we started talking we clicked and ended up sharing an apartment together the following year. Amy was like the best friend I'd never met. Somehow it no longer mattered that she was the rival blonde who stole my look! I didn't need to be first or best anymore.

Purple Jesus

Besides my grandmother, and an intense desire to stand out in a crowd, there were some other surprising influences on my personal tastes that stick with me to this day, including my brother Donnie.

For a few years in between working as a car detailer and running HAWGS-R-US. Donnie ventured into the stripper bar business. One of his body shop clients took a shine to him and offered him a job as a DJ at one of his clubs. Donnie being Donnie figured, *Why not?* The pay was a lot better, and even though he'd never spun a record in his life, he liked music and knew how to talk to people. The crowd loved his commentary as he introduced the girls, who were also fans. One stripper in particular, Susie, liked him so much she became Donnie's bride.

Donnie decided to get married in my paternal grand-mother's Lutheran church. Donnie, her first grandchild, was Nanny Vivian's favorite. As tall as she was round, she was the sweetest little lady and cooked the most delicious cakes and meals. But she was also a devout church lady. She was there every Sunday when the doors opened, and her social life revolved around her church. A God-fearing woman who read the Bible every night, Nanny was thrilled when Donnie told her he wanted to marry in her church. No matter what he did for a living, in her eyes he could do no wrong.

She loved Susie as well. We all did. But talk about rough. Every other word had four letters. Susie told us that one of the few honors she earned as a child was president of "the cussing club." She cursed in this growly voice, and thigh-high cutoff jeans, T-shirts, and flip-flops were her daily uniform. Meanwhile, Nanny's church was about as conservative as you could get. This was going to be interesting.

The wedding theme was purple. Purple, purple every-where, like some bordello out of the Old West, from the flowers to the ribbons to the party favors. Everyone wore deep plum purple in a satin that was shiny as a mirror, with shoes dyed to match. It was almost liquid, like grape juice turned into fabric. Even Donnie, who looked adorable with his freshly coiffed mullet, accented his all-white tuxedo with tails with a purple satin cummerbund and a matching bow tie.

All of the bridesmaids, save for myself and my first cousin, were strippers, and for some reason purple was their favorite color. They went on and on about how much they loved pur-ple. The dresses were cut low in the front and the back, kind of how you would expect stripper bridesmaids' dresses to look. I thought it would be hard to find bridesmaids outfits that were so low-cut, although the only one who was not flat chested was me. By the way they sashayed down the aisle, you could tell they'd walked more than a few runways in the past. Little Miss seventeen-year-old Prisspot (i.e., me) was mortified.

Susie wore a white *quinceañera* dress that she bought off a Mexican friend whose daughter had just turned fifteen. It had an open sweetheart neckline with an open back, cut almost down to her butt crack, and tier after tier of ruffles—stripper on top and wedding meringue on the bottom. The problem was that Susie had a huge tattoo on her chest, and the dress was too low cut to cover it up. Susie had a few tattoos, including a rose and a butterfly, long before it was considered acceptable. We noticed it right before the wedding ceremony, and I scrambled to cover it up with makeup, but it took a lot of layers. If Nanny had seen it, she would have climbed under the church pew.

As a side note, one of Susie's stepbrothers, who was in the wedding party, had to be hidden until the last minute because there was a warrant out for his arrest. His ex-wife, one of the bridesmaids, had gone after him for failing to pay child support, but there was no way he was going to miss out on this moment. They had to be separated for the whole ceremony.

As the guests were filing out of the church pews, the father of the bride—well, more of a father figure, a sweet man who had been one of her mother's boyfriends—got up and linked arms with one of the ushers. He'd seen the guy doing it for the women as they were leaving the church and just assumed it was part of the drill. The poor man didn't get out much.

At this point, everyone in my family was in hysterics. On one side of the church the bride's family looked like the Beverly Hillbillies, showing up at the church in T-shirts, jeans, and cutoffs. On the other side was our family, Nanny, the proper Southern Baptist matron, and all of her church lady friends.

"Oh my gosh, Nanny is going to go over the edge," Patrick said. "She'll never recover!"

But, wait, there was more. At the reception, which was held in a country club across town, my brother had rented a huge champagne fountain. Instead of champagne, he stuck to the color theme and turned it into a huge Purple Jesus fountain, which is a combination of Everclear, vodka, grape juice, and ginger ale. He made it extra fancy with some fruit slices floating around in the bowl. Donnie's limo driver, "Blade," drank most of it and had to be carried back to his limousine at the end of the reception. Donnie drove him home.

The next day Mammaw Betty called.

"I'm dying, I'm dying!"

"What's wrong, Mammaw?" I asked her.

"I'm so ill. Come and take me to the hospital, now!"

We rushed over and she could barely stand up. She'd been throwing up all morning and looked ashen, so we asked her if she'd eaten anything for breakfast.

"No, nothing. Just the fruit from the wedding reception last night."

Mammaw was drunk. That fruit would have soaked up

all the Purple Jesus alcohol, which was about as intense as moonshine, but she didn't know any better. She was a teetotaler and had never been tipsy a day in her life.

And that's why the color purple has always been another don't. That whole wedding theme will forever be associated in my mind with trailer trash. The marriage itself lasted for twenty-two years. This past Thanksgiving, Donnie and Susie announced they were getting divorced, although they are still the best of friends; they continue to have dinner together every night and Donnie's new "man cave" sits just one hundred yards from her trailer. It was the kindest, most loving breakup I have ever witnessed.

I love Donnie and Susie both dearly, but hearing those bridesmaids go on and on about how much they loved those dresses horrified me. They couldn't wait to wear them again, and I couldn't wait to take mine off. I kept the dress, because in my world throwing out a bridesmaid's dress is sacrilege. For years afterward it hung in the back of my closet, and there it stayed. The whole experience gave me an aversion to that hue I will never shake. Purple and butterflies, because of the stripper tattoos. . . .

The Lolly Look

But I do love pink, lime green, aqua, and orange—colors that pop in crisp patterns with precious details like ruffles, trims, and bows. Colors and prints have to match, without trying too hard. And I like prints with Scottie dogs, turtles, cars, boats, and anchors—anything retro or fun. All of my life experiences, good and bad, have been poured into LWD's look, which is feminine, aspirational, and fresh, with its own quirky kind of charm. It's also practical. Simplicity is key.

It all started with a desire to recreate the lost innocence of childhood. I was a girl of the '70s, long before kids had cell phones and the Internet, when everyone played outside. We dressed up for family holidays and occasions that were made even more special with the fun and festive outfits we wore. Sadly, I think mine was the last generation in which kids could be kids and childhood lasted for several years beyond kindergarten. Maybe I'm biased, but I don't think we were anywhere near as precocious back then. Well into our tween years, we dressed up in wholesome, child-appropriate attire. We weren't trying to look like the latest YouTube star. We wore bright colors, ruffles, and ribbons. We aimed to be cute, not sexy.

Part of my inspiration for Lolly Wolly Doodle was born out of frustration. Sunday was the day our family would get dressed up and go to church, but when I tried shopping for my daughters' outfits, as well as my own, nothing affordable had the look I wanted for my girls. It was tough to find clothes for me that were roomy and comfortable, not too tight but with enough fit to feel feminine and pretty. And the options for little girls were limited to mommy mini-me's, in styles too grown up and revealing for a toddler or a little girl, in the tackiest colors and patterns. I wanted something classic and sweet. Where were the cute smock dresses and pinafores that I wore as a kid? Oh yeah, my mother and my childhood BFF, Mammaw Betty, an expert seamstress who stitched together entire suits for my grandfather sewed them for me.

Then one Mother's Day Will bought me a sewing machine so that I could whip up these innocent, classic looks for Vivi and Bella. I liked this gift better than anything he'd ever given me, even my car, because it gave me the creative outlet I'd been craving. Will once asked me whether I would ever use it, because he didn't want to waste money. Now he boasts it's the best investment he ever made.

The designs I came up with were simple, because that's all I had the skill set to sew. The earlier designs had very few darts or pleats, and we only introduced zippers recently. When we went out to dinner as a family, people would openly admire the clothes and asked me where I got them. Since I had some leftover fabric, I figured I would make some extras to sell, and soon I was spending what little free time I had stitching together scraps of material in the corner of my bedroom.

Our motto was simple: Let kids be kids. Give moms access to something age appropriate, affordable, and adorable. We launched during the recession, but what drove me to put stuff online was the fact that, as dressed down as mothers were, their kids were always dressed up. Things were hitting hard everywhere, but whenever I went to a mall or a restaurant I could see how hard they were trying to give their children a sense of pride in their appearance, even if it was just a cute hair bow or a brightly colored tee.

I got it. As a mom I would stop spending on my own wardrobe, but never my children's. I always wanted them to look good. When someone saw Bella dressed up and said, "Oh, she is so adorable, where did you get that?" I'd feel a sense of pride, even if I had spit-up in my hair. Someone just acknowledged how cute my daughter was. It was the biggest compliment you could give me, and I knew that's how most mothers would feel. Two years later we decided to dress the sweat pants–clad moms, and now our ladies' line makes up 70 percent of our business. As the economy improved, they wanted to match their kids' cuteness.

The level of kids' clothes we were producing could cost upwards of eighty dollars in the children's boutiques, which sold brands like Bonpoint, Alex and Alexa, or Petit Bateau. I simply couldn't afford to pay that much for a smock dress and have Bella ruin it the first time she wore it by spilling a glass of orange juice, and I knew I wasn't alone. I wanted to give my customers these same people-stopping, comment-inducing outfits but make them so affordable they could buy them in multiples. To achieve this, I had to take a pattern idea and simplify it. When I had the factory, we had to figure out how a design could be produced quickly and cheaply, without sacrificing quality, cuteness, or fit. But that didn't stop us from being creative. **Sometimes true innovation is easier when you're forced to work inside some lines.** It was a constant balancing act of creativity and manufacturing capability, based on what fabrics were available. It was a marriage of necessity and imagination, with lots of tweaking along the way.

The Right Fit

My other focus was fit. Most brands design for a standardized ideal that doesn't exist anymore. Because of my own body shape—petite build up top with a wider butt—it's always been hard for me to find well-fitting clothes that I love. When you go shopping and cannot find anything that is flattering, you don't feel good about yourself. It happens to me every time. It's also hard to shop online when you never have time to return anything. Sizing in designer clothes tend to be all over the place. You might wear a size 0 in one item and a size 6 in another.

So we paid a lot of attention to sizing, starting with our own body shapes, at the sizes that usually work for us. Yes, we used mannequins to measure to industry standards, but we worked hard so that everything we carry fit in the same way. We didn't want our customers to have to play a guessing game. And if a particular style did fit small, we called it out and let them know they might want to order up a size or two.

When you do create something, remember who it's for. We wanted our moms to feel good about themselves. Erica, one of our designers, made me aware of how important it was to have larger sizes, or to build in options for longer lengths and wider shoulder straps. Our customers also inspired us to offer a broader range of styles and fit for larger women. Our most popular size for women has always been extra large, and our least popular size is extra small. That's just how real American women are built. When we put up our first ladies' tunic in extra large, we had a huge outpouring of requests to go even bigger.

"There is nothing on the market like this," they would write. "Don't forget us, please."

"I can't find anything to match my daughter for the family Christmas pictures."

"I don't want to wear solid colors in a tent. I want to wear bright prints in fun styles. I want to look trendy too."

Now we go all the way up to 3X. It's challenging, because the smaller body types have fewer shape configurations. The larger you are, the more variations there can be. But when we get it right for our customers, we are rewarded. Our palazzo pants are a case in point. They wash well, they are comfortable, and they are slimming, with a nice flow, no matter what your body type. People order them in multiples, so if something works, it doesn't go away before the end of a season. We bring it back in all kinds of iterations.

Growth Spurt

We have also had to adapt to the variations in standard children's sizes. Kids are growing much faster these days. I don't know whether it's the hormones they are putting in processed foods or what, but at one Junior League show I met a four-year-old who was a girl's size 12. She wasn't overweight in any way. Just tall and solid for her age. But can you imagine how hard it is to find something age appropriate for a four-, five-, or six-year-old? Try buying them a pair of shorts that aren't cut so high around the butt cheek they look like underpants. That's the style these days even in the smallest sizes. I don't know what these retailers are thinking!

I'm not a strict mom, but I want my child to look appropriate. Let's get back to a little modesty for the women and girls who want it. The school dress code for shorts is mid-thigh, but that style and fit is so hard to find for the bigger girls that they have to resort to long pants or capris in the dead heat of a Southern summer. It's not right.

These girls also want to look like their friends, but you can't easily buy them a sweet A-line or cotton dress, and the proportions are different. That's why we quickly started going to a 10 and 12 in the girl's styles. They were larger sizes and cuts that looked extremely young, because they were still for children. And once you capture that customer, you have them for the next few years, because there is really nowhere else for them to shop.

It's why we never sweat the ankle biters. About a year into our success with Facebook, in 2011, there were so many children's clothing companies online, trying to do the same thing, taking orders and building communities through social media. But they didn't have the depth of customer engagement we enjoyed, and they lacked the same variety and quality. They produced things as cheaply as they could, sourcing in China and promising unrealistic delivery times, because when China says they'll ship in two to four weeks it actually takes twelve to sixteen. They were on a learning curve and trying to scale up too fast, and when Facebook sales collapsed, most of them disappeared.

Telling a Story

Not that they could have kept up with us anyway. As long as we stayed true to certain principles of style and fit, we could come up with dozens of new looks each week. *We stayed ahead by constantly tweaking. Not reinventing so much as adjusting with subtle changes that added up to some-thing fresh. True creativity never stays still.* Although we had certain design templates, a different fabric pattern here, a trim there would make any item we posted look brand-new.

Looking back, I realize I was always hitting reset on how I presented myself to the world. I was pushing the button on all of those old thrift-shop items, giving them new life, and I was reinventing my outfits with different combinations every day to make sure the other girls in school could never catch me. In retrospect, that was another way we took care of those relentless copycats.

The most fun way to stay fresh in the design process is to come up with new prints. We've since invested in and devel-oped proprietary technology and systems to design and print fabric that allows us to offer our own patterns on quality fabric that you can't find anywhere else. So now we don't have to depend on what's already out on the market (more on that later). Jackie, Erica, Amy, Brittany, and I, along with the rest of our design team, Katie McCree and Laney Smith, have complete freedom to indulge our creative side.

Keep your eyes open and your camera phone ready. Great ideas can come from anywhere. I tend to create by association. I love nothing more than to tell a story. When I see something, like a pink sundress splashed with green woodcut pineapples, I imagine it being worn to dinner on a family vacation in the Bahamas, which is my idea of heaven. I can look out at our pool house, notice the way the orange and turquoise cushions go together, or love the way some coral looks above the fireplace, and it will show up in one of our prints.

I get inspired by other designers, but only certain elements of their design. I recently discovered vintage Pucci and adore the deliciously bold graphics and rich colors. I don't like fine lines. Impressionist and abstract painters inspire me because they leave plenty of room for interpretation.

I love the flexibility that this new technology has given us. When I see something in my head, I can create it on the screen. I recently spent half a day designing a woodcut pineapple, and now it's a blockbuster. I can bring in a piece of wrapping paper, point out a painting, describe a theme, and it's like Christmas when my design team comes back to me with some ideas they've put together on our computer-aided design program.

I nix fabrics that remind me of my grandmother's couch or patterns that have become ubiquitous and stale, like chevron. If I don't feel it's us, or not our color wave, I'll pull the plug. But it's not all about what I like. Members of my team regularly bring me tear outs from magazines or fabric swatches from their closets. Sometimes they'll even bring in their children's or grandchildren's favorite dresses. And of course my daughters, Vivian and Eva Bella, have their own ideas for a Lolly look and inspire me every day. *Just because you haven't come up with the idea yourself, don't dismiss it. No one person has authority, but all together we do.* I try to stay humble enough to recognize that I am not always right, and that Lolly Wolly Doodle employees and customers are so steeped in the brand that their ideas can be winners too.

My tastes have evolved as I've listened to others. More than once, my design team has proven me wrong with a home run on something I hated. One of my favorite lines in the history of our company, a coral print, had sales that were just okay when we released it. The same thing happened with our shell line, which I expected to go like gangbusters. But our scrolling medallion line, which wasn't my favorite, had fantastic sales.

We are constantly evolving as we broaden our customer reach beyond the South while still staying true to our core Lolly look. I'm still recognizable, but I'd say I am much less rigid than the high school version of myself. I will always hate purple, but today I make an exception for lavender. I'll even allow a rare butterfly to flutter through.

AH-HA'S

- There will always be copycats. When you are successful, imitation is a fact of life.
- When you pour your heart and soul into what you do, you don't need to obsess about being the first or the only person to do something.
- Not everyone is struck by lightning, but you do have your own unique fingerprint. You own a collection of life experiences and impressions that no one else has, and that can bring a flavor and feeling to anything if you put your all into what you are creating.
- If it is what you love and need to be doing, you can't help but make it unique in countless subtle ways that add up to something truly special.
- Anyone can be creative. It's all about finding a solution to a problem, then taking action.
- Don't watch what anybody else is doing too closely. You can be inspired by great work, but never consciously imitate. At the same time, the worst thing you can do is focus too hard on originality. Worry less about being original and more about being authentic.
- Sometimes true innovation is easier when you're forced to work inside some lines. LWD's design process was a constant balancing act of creativity and manufacturing capability, based on what fabrics

were available. It was a marriage of necessity and imagination, with lots of tweaking along the way.

• We stayed ahead by tweaking. Not reinventing so much as adjusting with subtle changes that added up to something fresh. True creativity never stays still. Although we had certain design templates, a different fabric pattern here, a trim there would make a certain item we posted look brand new.

• Keep your eyes open and your camera phone ready. Great ideas can come from anywhere.

• Just because you haven't come up with the idea yourself, don't dismiss it. No one is an authority.

Five

Know When to Grow

The reason the windshield is so large and the rearview mirror is so small is because what's happened in your past is not near as important as what's in your future.

–JOEL OSTEEN

L ess than two years after that first fateful meeting with Shana, our year-on-year growth was 700 percent, with Facebook likes reaching close to a million. To put that in perspective, Zappos Labs, one of the most tech-savvy e-commerce businesses in existence, had 1.5 million Facebook fans, and they were a much larger company. JCPenney, which launched its Facebook presence with a lot of fanfare, eventually withdrew its sales operations from the site. So we were succeeding where others were failing—and breaking e-commerce records.

Neck deep in hiring and keeping up with orders, I was completely unaware of it at the time, but the technology world was beginning to buzz about what we were doing. One business magazine put Lizzy and me on their list of "30 Startup People to Watch This Year." Magazines I'd never heard of were mentioning our name. Will Young, the director of Zappos, was telling our story every chance he got. He first heard of us at a retail conference in Germany, from an analyst who'd heard about us from a venture capitalist in New York. We were being used as a case study at global technology conferences as far away as Australia. We were circling the globe and didn't even know it. Then came another phone call from New York.

"You are starting to pop up on peoples' radars," Shana told me. "I think it's time."

"Time for what?" I asked.

"Time you went after that second round of investors."

"Why? We don't need the money."

"Because in the business world you take the money when you're hot to grow and scale faster, *not* when you need it. I'll make a few calls."

"But I can't leave the factory—we're so busy!"

"You've got Lizzy. You've got your team. If you can't leave for a couple of days without worrying the place will go up in flames, something is wrong. Brandi, you're a business leader. Now go out there, lay on that Southern belle charm of yours, and be the face of your brand!"

I didn't believe we needed the extra cash from investors, but it couldn't hurt to put ourselves out there. Now I was one of Lexington's largest employers. My Doodle family had grown to more than 200 members. We'd gotten so big that, by September 2012, we'd moved out of our Leonard Road headquarters into a 19,000-square foot facility on Piedmont Road, a former medical-equipment warehouse. We received a state grant to gut the place and fit it out for our ever-expanding factory.

We were thrifty, made high margins on our sales, and were always reinvesting revenues, keeping next to no inventory and wasting nothing. I Dumpster dived more than once to salvage bags full of our discarded scraps when we'd run out of fabric for a particularly popular item. But eventually we'd need to scale up, buy more equipment, build a leading tech team to improve infrastructure, and increase volume, so it was decided that we should do a round of preemptive financing. ***You have to know when to grow.*** Many start-ups get stuck in that transition phase between the garage and a real live, grown-up business. If we were really going to do this, Shana was right. Now was the time.

The Lion's Den

One of the first meetings Shana arranged for us was at Facebook's headquarters in Palo Alto, California, an encounter that filled me with as much excitement as dread. It was because of the Facebook platform that we had been enjoying such phenomenal sales with little to no marketing overhead. But I never really did get to the bottom of whether my use of their platform was even allowed. The Facebook rules were never clear about conducting business through their newsfeed, so I took full advantage of this grey area. Technically, I know I probably wasn't supposed to sell on the site, but I got so hooked that I rationalized the decision. Doing what no one had done before meant it was wide open to interpretation. But in the back of my mind was the always the possibility that, once LWD caught the attention of one of the Facebook executives, our only real sales channel would be shut down. We were walking into the lion's den.

We figured our best hope was to convince Facebook that we could help each other. I was naïve enough to think I could do something for them. But we badly wanted their support. They could do things for us on the tech side, like opening more doors on the back end as we were automating and streamlining our sales platform. This could save us precious productive hours we could be spending on design, product development, branding. . . . Here we were, doing something sort of rogue, yet enabling e-commerce on a site everyone had been saying was just social. If they were ever going to become a viable platform for businesses, they could point to us as proof of concept. We were their ultimate case study, and we'd be willing to open our doors and share the story of how we did it in return.

When Lizzy and I walked into the lobby, I felt vaguely like an outlaw. We came early for the meeting, and, while we were waiting, someone I'd never seen before came up to me and said, "Oh my gosh, you're Lolly Wolly Doodle!"

Someone all the way out in Silicon Valley knew *me*?

"Yes sir?" I replied, looking at him quizzically.

"You're Brandi!

"I am!"

"I've been trying so hard to get in touch with you!"

It was Chris Bennett, the CEO and cofounder of Soldsie, an e-commerce start-up based in San Francisco that was apparently inspired by what we were doing. Chris and his partner launched Soldsie in May 2012, allowing other businesses to monetize their social media pages through the use of comments—exactly what we were doing. Soldsie helped retailers to upload their products according to a template that included the price and item description, and then schedule campaigns and sales according to their chosen schedules. It could track customers, allow them to wait-list for out-of-stock items, and turn Facebook and Instagram into points of sale, just as we had already been doing for two years. In effect, they created a brand-new e-commerce platform, then took it several steps beyond, just by watching what we were doing!

You never really know the full impact or scope of your actions on the rest of the world. I loved the fact that we were inspiring other entrepreneurs to take a leap. I didn't feel quite so out of place anymore.

Lizzy and I were escorted to the office of someone who was supposedly pretty high up the chain, an executive vice president (although everyone is an EVP of something at Facebook). I found myself babbling at this man, doing my utmost to be impressive, flattering, and engaging all at once. He was both courteous and dismissive, barely looking up from his iPhone.

"Oh that's great!" he said. "We're so happy to meet you."

They were just polite noises, but I persisted, telling him about a sale we had just posted and the responses on our newsfeed that were streaming in real time. Suddenly he stopped texting and looked up from his darn cell phone, eyes wide.

"Wait, what? How do you sell?" he asked.

"We only sell on Facebook," I told him, a lump forming in my throat.

"_How_ do you sell on Facebook?"

"On our newsfeed." I explained, beginning to regret what I'd said and figuring we were in big trouble now.

"What do you mean on your newsfeed?"

I flipped my laptop around to show him a wall full of comments. It was reckoning time. This could be the moment that ended it all. But when he saw my screen he seemed more curious and excited than outraged that we were breaking the rules.

"What are all those comments?" he asked me.

"Sales. Those are people trying to buy what we have, but we don't have enough, we can't sell as much as people want."

"How many items do you have for sale?"

"About thirty dresses, but 200 people are trying to buy them."

You could practically see the light bulb flicking on in his head. He immediately started calling in other executives to share the news and show them our page.

"This is amazing!" he said. "We've never seen anything like this before!"

Toward the end of that conversation I mustered up the courage to finally ask him, "Are we breaking the rules?"

He had to think for a minute. Technically, we were not, because I was not executing the sale in the newsfeed, merely talking about the items we had for sale. Our customers were expressing the interest to buy in the Facebook newsfeed, but no one was executing transactions. Because the invoicing and payments were taking place through another site, PayPal, we were fine. Talk about relief! It was an exhale moment.

By the time Lizzy and I left Palo Alto, the tech world was buzzing about our tiny Southern start-up with the precious name. LWD had become the golden unicorn of e-commerce everyone was looking for. Facebook was interested in us after all, to show that business could be done on the platform. They offered us support in the form of publicity, contacts, even a dedicated page manager. They also had a couple of case studies written about the Doodle. The hot topic was how to make money off Facebook, so it was an easy story to sell. Through them, we got our first major media coverage. *CBS This Morning* did a segment called "North Carolina Mom Turns Hobby into Facebook Success." We'd gone national.

White Trash

More doors opened, and the phone wouldn't stop ringing. I started speaking at business schools and CEO conferences around the country. Lizzy and I decided to divide and conquer. She rustled up her venture capitalist contacts for face-to-face meetings while I told my story in front of the influential business audiences that invited me to speak. Venture capitalists invest in small to medium-sized businesses they think have promise, in the belief that their money will help take it to the next level, with the ultimate goal of either selling the whole company at a sizeable profit or sharing in the dividends. At some stage in the development of your business, you may need to partner with one or a few of these savvy individuals, and we'd already reached that point in Lolly Wolly Doodle's growth story. Of course I hated spending that time away from my kids, but that's what I'd signed up for.

Finding the right investors isn't as straightforward as

you would think. It's not just about getting their money. Every dollar is not created equal. They have to believe in what you are doing and be the right fit; otherwise, their investment can be more of a burden than a blessing. The results of those initial meet and greets were mixed. Lizzy described what we were doing to one group of investors in Boston and pointed out our unique customer base–the middle of the country and the South. Most e-commerce companies tend to get most of their business from the coastal areas, so part of the appeal to investors should have been the fact that we were capturing this huge underserved population.

"It really is the white space of e-commerce," she told them.

One of the investors quipped, "You mean the white trash of e-commerce?"

We had a little more luck when we met with Steve Case, the cofounder and former CEO of America Online, and Donn Davis, a former president and COO at AOL. Since his retirement from AOL–Time Warner, Steve had gone on to invest millions into Zipcar, LivingSocial, Revolution Money, HelloWallet.... He and Donn then cofounded Revolution LLC, a $450 million venture capital fund, to make early bets on Internet companies that showed promise. Lolly Wolly Doodle hit his radar when the sister of one of their junior associates, one of our most enthusiastic customers, raved about us.

Soon after that encounter, Steve and Donn took a tour of the factory, fell in love with our Made in the USA story, and wooed us until we accepted their $20 million investment. They got us even more press when they told the world they expected us to reach a billion-dollar valuation (short lived as that was)! Much as he was impressed by the way we had solved the Facebook conundrum, he appreciated the innovative way we integrated our manufacturing process and supply chain with our customers' social media cues. He saw possibilities in what we were doing beyond children's clothing.

What was truly revolutionary about what we were doing was the way we were using the social media feedback loop to amass information about what works in order to make smarter design and sales decisions, and configure our operations accordingly. Typically, we would make up samples, post them on Facebook, and produce them only in the sizes that people ordered, so there would be no overstock. Then we would compare the sales of that product with previous designs to see if it was a winner. If it was, we would either mass-produce it and keep the surplus to sell on our LWD website, or create new product "pods," going deeper into that style template to create a collection, with different fabrics, necklines, or trims. The variations would be limited to keep production simple. And the more customer feedback, or what the industry calls "predictive analytics," we got, the better decisions we could make, enabling us to design our operations with even more efficiency. It meant we were able to introduce more than a dozen SKUs a day, which kept our customers excited and engaged.

What Steve and Donn saw was a manufacturing and e-commerce model that could translate across industries. By knowing our customer so well and refining the way we communicated with them, we were taking the guesswork out of merchandising. As Donn described it, I was "reinventing apparel much as Dell reinvented the PC industry. It's afford-able custom in real time with little inventory risk."

To see what I'd been doing through Donn's eyes felt em-powering. *When you are just putting one foot in front of the other, doing whatever is necessary, take a moment to lift up your head and see where you are. It can be enlightening to step back and see your situation from a broader perspective.*

Of course, a deal like that was big news in the tech and investment community. Once Revolution announced its lat-est bet, more investors took interest, including those Bosto-nians Lizzy had met with earlier. That seems to be the way with venture capital: Money attracts money. Some lackey on their team wrote an e-mail to me, reintroducing himself, con-gratulating us on our news, and asking for a meeting. When I asked Lizzy about him and she reminded me of their con-versation. I couldn't resist.

"Yes, of course I remember you!" I e-mailed in reply. "You're the ones who called our customers white trash. No thank-you!"

Lizzy was bowled over that I had the nerve to call them out like that. These were powerful people. But I couldn't resist, if only to get her reaction and make her bust out laughing.

Upgrades

I finally got over my reluctance to spend other people's money (at a cost I will tell you more about later). If I was going to buy into the dream that we could go even bigger, I believed

I had to. We were already busting out of our second location, so we leased an 80,000-square-foot warehouse and shipping hub across town—a huge space about the size of three football fields.

Beyond that, we had to invest a lot more into our technology infrastructure. Lizzy had already helped us improve many aspects of our sales, branding, and customer service. When she first arrived, she saw a mess. We were struggling to keep up with customer orders. Every day the UPS truck would back up to our steel gate and pick up a mountain of packages in white plastic envelopes. We hadn't even bothered to brand our shipping materials. Who had time?

Back then, at the beginning of 2012, our customers' e-mails went unanswered for too long. We were so overwhelmed, it was about playing catch-up, and customer service suffered. As Lizzy pointed out, we could never take them for granted. *If we had any hope of sustained success, we had to cultivate repeat business.* A late shipment or a rushed exchange with a mom who was worried about not getting her July 4th family photo outfits shipped out on time could cost us a customer, and her friends. *We couldn't afford to fall short. We had to give her an experience that exceeded her expectations.* It was one of the biggest challenges of real-time, customized production.

Before Lizzy came along we were like a race car hurtling to the finish line: going fast, winning the race for now, but losing windshield wipers and hubcaps along the way. It wasn't pretty. But the upside was that we had a lot of room to grow, and if we could reach that capacity, it meant a lot more customers, more sales, and more profits. That's what made investors so excited—we had so many ways we could scale up that the sky was the limit. At $10 million in sales by the end of two years, we were just getting started.

But first we had to find a way to communicate our core values and show customer appreciation at every touch point. Not only did I need to be more of a figurehead for the brand, we needed to build a better website and make some drastic upgrades to the flow of communication with our customers, our manufacturing, and our supply chain. As it was, our technology infrastructure simply wasn't scalable. It couldn't keep up with our growth. This wasn't my area of strength, and Laura, the former forklift driver, had taken us as far as she was able to. She was patching things together as best she could, and what she had done with limited resources was incredible, but Lizzy had to explain to me there was a difference between IT and engineering.

Every business needs an IT person to make sure the server is working and provide technical and administrative support for the computer systems. But a true e-commerce company has to be much more sophisticated. They need experienced software engineers who can speak a completely different language of symbols and numbers, or binary code. Without them, there would be nothing to support. It's the engine and intelligence that makes the whole thing run. We needed engineers to build a sales and manufacturing system at the professional level of something you would find in New York or San Francisco. It was time to find somebody to get us from here to there, and Lizzy had just the guy: Angad Singh.

From Bombay to Boondocks

Lizzy and Angad had worked together at a major tech start-up before joining forces at Lolly Wolly Doodle. They didn't know each other well, but they shared mutual respect from a distance and always wanted to work together again. Angad had learned through a friend that Lizzy was looking for a chief technology officer to join our team at LWD, so he reached out to her. Making that connection was by far the biggest gift she gave me, beyond her own mentorship and sisterhood.

Angad was the kind of technology genius who could build something out of nothing. He possessed a killer combination of skills, knowledge, and imagination. He was the missing piece, exactly who we needed on the Doodle team. We had to work fast to build custom real-time manufacturing into our ERP system, and there was no such technology in existence that could be integrated with our customer feedback until he created it for us, from scratch.

But I have to admit I was worried. Initially Angad was going to have to spend a lot of time down in Lexington as he worked with Jordan and familiarized himself with our operations, and he was certainly different from what everyone around here was used to seeing.

Although self-described as more "spiritual" than religious, Angad is a Sikh, which means he wears a customary beard and turban. Sikhism is a centuries-old religion originating in South Asia that has nothing to do with Islam. If anything, its emphasis is on meditation, and its precepts are based on equality, selfless service, social justice, and honesty. It is a highly tolerant faith. Not that Angad was particularly religious. He just wore the trappings out of family tradition and cultural pride.

But it meant a lot of extra pat downs at the airport and funny stares wherever he went. I was paranoid that some of our local rednecks might confuse him with an Islamic extremist. More than once I caught a few glares as Angad and I sat down for lunch at our local barbecue place (he passed on the pulled pork and ordered chicken). But folks around here haven't been exposed to a lot outside of Davidson County lines, and a trip to Myrtle Beach is about as far as they've ever gone in the world, so there was a risk that their lack of worldliness might lead to some incorrect assumptions. They wouldn't be the first to call him "Osama."

When I asked him about it, he just shrugged and said, "I'm so obviously foreign, so I guess it's to be expected. You have to have a thick skin to deal with this world."

Our corner of the globe did come as a shock to Angad, but not because of the local attitudes so much as the fact that he was used to a more urban lifestyle. Born in Bombay, he left behind his sister and parents to do his master's in computer science at the Boston University in 2007 before moving to New York as one of the most sought-after geniuses among technology start-ups. He fit in well in the tech-geek environments of the East and West Coasts. After the success of his previous employer, he could have worked anywhere, but he chose us because, like Lizzy, he loved the idea of helping a company that was actually producing something real.

"All those cool social media apps felt so remote," he later

told me. "You can't see how you are making a difference in people's lives, if any."

His friends told him he was crazy to leave his glamorous, high-tech job for a children's clothing company "in the middle of nowhere." But, coming from India, Angad knew what it was like for families to struggle through poverty, so working with a business that was actually creating jobs in the middle of a recession was a huge incentive for him. Lizzy tried to prepare him for what he was in for. She told him we were raw as far as our technology went, and that he would have to build from the ground up, but instead of being put off, the challenge excited him.

He might have had second thoughts when he first came to our factory in February 2012. On the hour-and-a-half drive from the airport, he passed lot after lot of shuttered warehouses. Shops were closed, "For Sale" signs were stuck in front of property after property. Lexington looked like a ghost town. He was disturbed by the lack of tall buildings, disoriented by all the nature and open spaces, and completely confused by the rusted-out cars and car seats on the front lawns.

"Oh my God," he told Lizzy. "This is an America I have never seen before!"

Then he saw our "We Are Hiring" sign like a beacon by the driveway, and a parking lot crammed full of cars. When he walked through our doors, he saw a hive of activity. The first thing that struck him was the sight of people actually making things with their hands. He walked around the sewing floor, beaming.

"This is such a happy place!" he said. "I love the industrial energy. I've never felt this before!"

He got to work right away, refining the system that Laura had helped us to set up because, as he told me, "I don't believe in trashing whatever was there before. The newest is not necessarily the best."

It was working for us, up to a point. But Angad added better and more scalable features, like the capacity to see who exactly was liking our page and posts. That information was like gold to us. Facebook wouldn't reveal the profile of who was liking us and wasn't readily providing real-time data, so we would put up sales and take them down without knowing enough about our customer engagement. Angad worked like a hacker, loving every bit of his rebelliousness as he peeked inside the matrix and figured it out. By the time he was finished, even the folks at Facebook couldn't quite understand what he did and frequently called on him for advice.

With a little guidance from Lizzy and me, Angad was able to size up the needs of our operation almost immediately. He started developing a custom software that would better structure our design and sales data, and allow the supply chain, cutting and sewing operations, and warehouse to be reorganized so that each piece of the fabric moved through production as quickly and efficiently as possible. We were already speedy, but there was room for improvement, especially when it is all too easy for things to fall apart as you grow. Every minute shaved off production time was an increase in volume and orders going out the door.

To support all of these new software systems, Angad set up a team of top engineers in India and the United States. He knew and trusted them, and by leveraging his relationships back home he was able to make communication with them seamless and cost effective. They charged a fraction of what engineers in the States got paid and made it possible to build a tech team more quickly given the severe shortage of engineering talent here. Now we had contractors in Bombay and offices in New York! We still did most of our production in Lexington, but we'd outsourced some of the more ever-green, popular designs in cotton knits to China, and our smocked goods to El Salvador. From our little suburban ga-rage we'd grown into a worldwide operation!

Cover Girl

Lolly Wolly Doodle was cooking. Our growth was phenom-enal, I had the backing of the stars of venture capital, people I trusted in my corner, and a business that was raking in rev-enues as we built in a smarter infrastructure. Suddenly the business media wasn't just talking about me, they were talk-ing *to* me. Facebook's publicity firm, along with Zappos's Andrew Young, who told the world he had an "e-commerce crush" on us, gave us more national exposure, bringing *Good Morning America* to our doorstep for a story about Made in the USA manufacturing called "America Strong." Reporters from *Bloomberg* and *Reuters* called for quotes. Then Tom Foster, the writer at *Inc.* I mentioned earlier, flew down from New York to do an in-depth feature on us.

It went well. So well, in fact, that in the early spring of 2014 I got a call from one of the editors asking me whether I would be available the next day to do a cover shoot. There would be no guarantees that my story would land on the front, but their previous pick had been difficult and wouldn't cooperate for the photographer. I happened to be in New York that week for meetings with our board, so the timing was perfect. Locked away after all those years of getting married and raising babies, the former beauty pageant queen inside me broke out with a roar!

But what was I going to wear? They wanted me to bring several outfits to the shoot, and I'd only packed enough clothes for a couple of days. It was a great excuse to go shopping, but with that plus hair and makeup, I needed help. Lizzy had to leave me for a high school reunion, so I asked Katie Novak, my assistant, to come to New York. I bought her a ticket for the first available flight, at noon, and told her we'd make an evening of it.

Girl Friday

When I first met Katie she was dating my son, Kade. That relationship didn't last more than a couple of weeks, but Katie stayed because she fell in love with my two daughters and the beginnings of the Doodle. Growing up she didn't have much of a family life, so she adopted ours. I taught her how to monogram, and since then she has learned to jump in and help in any area of the business. She's my girl Friday, and she steps in to drive my daughters to and from school or to appointments when I'm too busy.

While I was waiting for Katie to arrive in New York, I started shopping. Lizzy gave me a list of stores to hit: Zara,

Ann Taylor, Theory.... I spent up a storm in Ann Taylor, but once I got to the checkout, my credit card was declined. I'd forgotten to tell the bank I was traveling. I used my personal card, bought armloads of stuff at Zara, the fast-fashion retailer we'd been compared to a lot in the press. I'd never been there before and was impressed by their merchandising. When I got to the checkout, the same thing happened. But that bank called me to check the transaction. They reinstated my card, but to pay for the Zara stuff I had to run out and find an ATM to pay cash.

I was exhausted, stressed, and the stores were closing. I still didn't have Spanx, hose, or shoes. And no Katie. While I was shopping like a crazy woman she called me in tears several times. The plane's landing gear had broken off, and they had to divert her flight to an airport with a longer runway, in Philadelphia. As she was landing she was hysterical. She thought she was going to die! Once on the ground, she Skyped to show me the fire trucks surrounding her plane. The poor girl didn't make it to our hotel until midnight.

The next morning, I had butterflies. I couldn't let down these nice people at *Inc.* just because I wasn't properly accessorized! After breakfast I sent Katie off to buy me some pantyhose and shoes while I was getting hair and makeup done, then we made our way to a beautiful Tribeca loft where the studio was located.

The photographer, Andrew Eccles, and his assistants could not have been more gracious. They asked me what music I liked (India Arie), set up the lights, primped my hair, and powdered my nose. All that pampering and deferential treatment made me feel like a movie star. The photographer got me to relax by telling me stories about some of the high-profile, high-maintenance people he'd photographed in the past–none by name of course. I could tell he had enough juicy celebrity gossip to fill a book. We joked around, playing with different poses, trying on the different outfits I'd bought. He snapped something sexy, to send to my husband.

"Look at you, you're a natural!" he told me, and showed me the unretouched photo on his screen. It was the best I've ever looked–a real confidence booster for a mom pushing forty!

They asked me to pull out some of the other dresses I'd bought, one of which was a pale pink shift with three-quarter bell sleeves. It was my favorite by far, but everyone shook their heads. "There's no way we can have this Southern Barbie on the cover of a business magazine wearing a pink dress," the editor later confessed to saying at an editorial meeting.

After a few more snaps, the photographer had me try it on anyway, just for the heck of it. It turned out to be the best photo of the entire shoot. It was our cover.

Hard Landing

When I got back to Lexington, it was back to reality with a thud. Facebook had changed its algorithms, and our monthly sales dropped from $1.2 million a month to $500,000 to roughly $50,000 within six months

We knew the easy ride was coming to an end. It had to. We had estimated it would take Facebook at least six months to a year to phase in their pay-to-play platform. If the move hadn't been so abrupt, we would have had just enough run-way to put some alternative marketing and sales channels in place without seeing such a sharp fall in revenues. The change affected a lot of businesses, and many less established e-commerce companies were wiped out overnight.

In our heyday, anything we posted on Facebook could go viral, and there was no limit to how many pairs of eyeballs could see what we were trying to sell. But Facebook drasti-cally cut the reach we had, making it necessary to run ex-pensive paid ads in order to be seen by customers. Facebook gave us a taste, then got us hooked on their platform. We were like junkies, and now our dealer was telling us it was time to pay up. Not that I blame them one bit. It's just smart business tactics. I'd have done the same thing in their posi-tion.

Ultimately it was my fault that we were blindsided. *I took things for granted, and complacency can kill a busi-ness.* I was so focused on revenue growth, increasing production, and getting the product shipped that I didn't adequately prepare. I was obsessed with hitting that top-line number and pleasing our new investors—almost to the exclu-sion of everything else. Yes, there were the distractions of de-mands from new investors and board members, but the buck stopped with me, because I made far too many assumptions. I didn't pull back or cut payroll fast enough. I didn't come up with a plan B for our marketing strategy. We were devel-oping platforms and creating apps for other social media platforms like Pinterest and Instagram, but there was no sense of urgency.

I have a tendency to get caught up in the here and now to

the detriment of long-term planning. That's my weakness. Maybe it's my squirrely ADHD brain. Or my OCD. Or both. I see something in front of me that needs to be done, like running a roll of fabric because I know I can do it faster and better than anyone else, and I get caught up in the moment when I should be sitting at my desk developing a strategy and execution plan for the weeks to come. If we are introducing a new line and the cutout pictures of the designs for our storyboard are jagged, the perfectionist in me will take them down and cut them straight. I can't stand it if one little thing is off. I fall down that rabbit hole, trying to fix something that I should be delegating to someone else, then I go blind to the larger vision.

The big question I should have been asking myself was, "Do I stay or do I go?" How long do you cling to what you know, what worked for you many times before? When do you make that break? Some people never get to find out, because they grow too comfortable with the old formula. This is one of the biggest challenges start-ups face as they grow. They get so preoccupied with what's in their rearview that they crash into the oncoming traffic. They think there's too much risk in changing things up when the opposite is true. Jack Welch was right when he said, "Change before you have to." *It takes a certain humility to recognize that you will never have it all figured out. But learning to let go is critical. As soon as you get too attached to a certain way of doing things, failure is inevitable.*

This is so true of e-commerce, especially when you rely on social media, where the shifts are constant. *A business is a living, breathing, evolving creature.* Today we still have to crack the Facebook code on an almost weekly basis, although with a greater focus on marketing than organic social engagement. Their engineers are constantly tweaking and experimenting with their algorithms, which has a ripple effect that can make the difference between having the winds at our backs or paddling furiously upstream. We eventually figured out that they make their changes on Tuesdays and Thursdays, like clockwork. It's as if the Facebook folks have these dials they set for likes, shares, and customer service, and all they do is stick in their fingers and jiggle them to the left or right.

It meant we had to get out ahead of it. I put a sticker on my computer monitor that read, "When there is no wind, we row." If we noticed something had changed, I'd lock myself in my office and dive deep into the research to figure out what they were doing. Then I'd get on the phone with Angad, who was a marketing genius who could do multiple data slices to come up with more ways we could read and reach our customers. Together, we figured out the shortcuts, until we had to start the process all over again. It was an ongoing saga, but eventually we realized it was a gift. Because no one else could figure out what Facebook was doing, it kept our competitors at bay.

The lesson here is that no one is special. When your business is built on someone else's mercy, they can take you to lunch every week, but there will never be any guarantees. Just like you shouldn't depend on a Walmart for all of your sales, you have to be willing to diversify. Today almost 100 percent of our revenues come from our website, but we still get a substantial percentage of our customer traffic through Facebook, which is now a paid platform.

God doesn't play favorites either. That *Inc.* cover represents my moment of hubris. I never did get to enjoy being on that cover, because by the time the issue was published, in June 2014, we were in the middle of Facebook fallout. When I heard it was on the newsstands, I couldn't even find a copy in my hometown. I had to scoop up every magazine on the shelf in the Charlotte airport bookstore.

"You must really love that magazine," the lady at the checkout said.

"Well, I kind of like the lady on the cover," I told her, holding up a copy next to my face.

"Oh, is that you?"

That's about as much recognition as I got. No one back home said much. We have a saying around here, "Don't let your head get so big it won't fit through the door."

Never again will I assume that I've cracked the code or permit myself to get cocky. As much as I wanted that moment to sit back, survey my queendom and think to myself, *I've got this*, **I had to face the fact that I will always be a work in progress.** God wasn't done with me yet. He had a few more hard lessons for me to learn.

AH-HA'S

- You have to know when to grow. It's easy to get stuck in that transition phase between the garage and a real live, grown-up business.
- Resist the temptation to cling to the same formula and stick to what worked before. We fear change, believing that we might somehow jinx ourselves if we stray off the well-worn path. But fear of change is the enemy of success. We should never allow ourselves to get too comfortable.
- Don't be surprised by who is watching. You never really know the full impact or scope of your actions on the rest of the world.
- Finding the right investors is not just about getting their money. Every dollar is not created equal. They have to believe in what you are doing and be the right fit; otherwise, their investment can be more of a burden than a blessing.
- When you are putting one foot in front of the other, doing whatever is necessary, take a moment to lift your head up and see where you are. It can be enlightening to step back and see the situation from a more holistic perspective.
- Cultivate repeat business for sustained success. A late shipment or a rushed exchange can cost a customer, as well as her friends. No one can afford to fall short,

so strive to give her an experience that exceeds her expectations.

- Never take success for granted. Complacency can kill a business.
- Ask yourself, "Do I stay or do I go?" How long do you cling to what you know, what worked for you many times before? When do you make that break? Some people never get to find out, because they get too comfortable with the old formula.
- "Change before you have to." As soon as you get too attached to a certain way of doing things, failure is inevitable.
- It takes a certain humility to recognize that you will never have it all figured out. But learning to let go of what's easy and familiar is critical.
- Because the shifts are constant, you have to be prepared to adapt at all times. A business is a living, breathing, evolving creature.
- No one is special. When your business is built on someone else's mercy, they can take you to lunch every week, but there will never be any guarantees, because they have to put their interests first.
- You are a work in progress, and that's a good thing. God will always have plenty of lessons to teach you.

Six

Cut to Be Kind

The truth of the matter is that you always know the right thing to do. The hard part is doing it.

–NORMAN SCHWARZKOPF

hings were tense on the Doodle floor. Every employee who got called into the office knew what it meant: They'd be out of a job by the day's end. Typically, I didn't involve myself directly in layoffs. I left it to Jamie or one of our department heads. It was one area of being a business leader I always struggled with, no matter what the circumstances. But if it was someone I knew well, delegating just didn't feel right. I had to put my big girl pants on and speak with them face-to-face. John Singleton, our vice president of operations and a brilliant retail executive, was one of them. We were not that far apart in age, but over the months we'd worked together, I began to think of him as a father figure. This was going to hurt.

John had taken us as far as he could with his more traditional retail background. He was a veteran of the industry

164 / BRANDI TEMPLE

who'd worked at JCPenney and Abercrombie & Fitch, and one of the many talents our board mandated that we hire. But we were like no other conventional retailer. His vast experience had minimal relevance to what we were doing at Lolly Wolly Doodle, and as time went by he recognized that too. The best he could offer was support by backing up our decisions to the board members and offering me tidbits of advice and encouraging stories to get me through the Facebook fiasco. His unwavering moral support meant everything to me, so when I was told to fire him less than a year later, I could barely spit the words out.

"John, I just wanted to say . . . ," I managed, before I started to bawl uncontrollably.

He put his arm around me and said, "I know, I know; you have to fire me. Please don't cry!"

"But I . . . I feel terrible about this!"

While I sat there sobbing, he basically fired himself.

"It's alright. You *have* to let me go. I'd do the same thing! It's one of the cuts you have to make. You're paying way too much for me. Honey, I'll be okay. I've got other offers lined up, and I can retire if I want to. I feel worse for you than I do for me. Please don't cry!"

I adored that man. But he was right. Firing him was part of the massive fallout we had to face after Facebook pulled the plug on us. We'd spent a fortune on payroll, and it was time to make some deep and painful cuts to get ourselves back on track. When revenues nose-dive, it exposes all of the inefficiencies. I would have been failing in my responsibility as a business leader if I hadn't drastically downsized.

Cruel to Be Kind

Leaders have to be prepared to make unpopular decisions. It's hard, but you can always build back up and hire again. I've always been the people pleaser, putting all of my energy into making people happy. But avoiding the unpleasantness, hurt feelings, and guilt risks killing the business. **Kindness in the short term can be selfish and negligent in the long term, because by then everyone is out of a job.** We ended up getting rid of about 40 people at a point when we had about 180 employed at the factory. It was gut wrenching. Apart from losing my Frannie, I can honestly say it was one of the darkest periods of my life.

We probably should have cut back long before the Facebook bubble burst. We had to let go of some good people, although many we hired had nothing to do, and a few were not the best workers, sauntering in late and always leaving the moment the clock ticked five. But that didn't make it any easier, and most were actually doing a great job. Several were close to me, including relatives. One was a young man I used to babysit. Another used to play baseball with Kade. He was always at our house, joining in on cookouts, dinners, and outings, like a member of our extended family.

His father, who owned a landscaping company, just happened to be working on the grounds by our pool at the time. Will and I were finishing up work on a house extension and brand-new pool area. It was a lengthy project that we'd spent years saving up for, and construction started well before the Facebook bubble burst, but it didn't look good that we were in the middle of home improvements just as the Doodle hit one of its deepest depressions. Like I said, in a small town, you live in a fishbowl. People gossip and make assumptions, and I was well aware of what they were thinking:

That Brandi, she took all the money out of the company to build herself a nice pool while we're suffering....

Not that I blame anyone. They didn't understand that I couldn't take money out of the company even if I wanted to. That's not how it works. I get a paycheck just like everyone else, and my check was a heck of a lot smaller than the salaries we were paying the people the board wanted me to hire.

It didn't help matters that members of my own family were the biggest gossips of all. My father, who is known as "Pops" by all the workers, comes into the factory a couple of times a week to help us make bows, although he's more like our company mascot, zipping around the floor in his electric scooter and chatting with everyone. Daddy is as bighearted as he is opinionated. He likes to get to know everyone on a deeper level, asking them about their problems and offering fatherly advice, so when there is any kind of cutback or a worker he is especially fond of doesn't get the hours she wants, I catch hell from him. He's made it his personal mission to recruit friends and neighbors who've fallen on hard times, and as far as he is concerned I could never pay them enough. He's like a one-man union.

Seeing the father of Kade's good friend toiling in my back-yard was a reminder of how close to home these layoffs were hitting. It felt like I'd let everybody down. Once again, I burst into tears, apologizing to the man, who could not have been more gracious.

"Brandi, he'll be okay," he told me. "You've got enough to worry about, so please don't go tearing yourself up about this." Kade's friend got a job at Lowe's the next day.

Another particularly brutal personnel change was Lizzy. She was my sanity. The board assigned each of us new roles within the organization because they wanted a leadership change and deemed that we "weren't going to get there from here" if we continued as co-CEOs. I was relegated to design, and Lizzy was asked to run business development by helping us to build powerful partnerships and a portfolio of potential buyers.

At first we were excited by the shift, because we could focus on our areas of strength and leave the corporate politics to someone else. We spoke about it a few times. "Oh my gosh, wouldn't it be nice?" we said. But, ultimately, Lizzy wasn't interested and decided to move on. It was like losing my best friend.

We called ourselves Thelma and Louise because we'd been so together on this crazy ride. We had grown so close over the previous two years that we could read each other's minds. Without her, I'd never have gotten through those endless, painful board meetings. We just had to look at each other, and one of us would start giggling. It'd be over. During one meeting, when everyone was busy texting and no one was listening to our concerns, I told them, "Oh yeah, last week I did a video on pole dancing. Turns out the Doodle moms are really excited about that."

No one except for Lizzy looked up. I said it to amuse her and keep the weight of the situation from drowning us. LWD was dying a death by a thousand cuts, but instead of stopping the bleeding, our board wanted to amputate. After those meetings we talked about all the things we'd like to do, like jumping up on the conference room table in the middle of a tense meeting and breaking out into a tap dance. We concocted fantasies about our retirement, when we would sit by the pool wearing T-shirts with the little blue Facebook thumbs-up symbols making a middle finger. Laughter was our coping mechanism during those dark times. When we were in triage mode after the Facebook fiasco, we did whatever we could to lighten the mood, like two kids who had to be separated in class.

But as much as we laughed together, we also worked shoulder to shoulder. Lizzy had put in the same eighty-hour work weeks as I had to correct course, aggressively building the business back up until revenues returned to their original levels. It took months of no sleep, working until our eyes bled, but we did it. I'd never met anyone so determined. She was full of grit. In many ways, I felt it was her company as much as mine.

In retrospect, I understand why she decided to move on. She was the queen of innovative tech start-ups, but now we were more of a brand than a platform. Her passion was for putting all the systems and infrastructure in place to get companies in the earliest stages off the ground. We were past that phase and had to transition to a more traditional e-commerce retail business. It took a while to rebound, and the investors didn't believe there was a clear enough vision for Lolly Wolly Doodle. That was entirely on me, although I selfishly wanted my partner in crime to stick around. Today she is living happily out West with her husband and children, thrilled to be far from the New York scene, working from home as she does what she enjoys most, launching innovative tech start-ups.

But when she left I lost my closest ally. I am seriously allergic to board meetings. Investor relations–flying to New York, reporting in on the latest numbers, stopping everything for an endless conference call–was not my thing, especially when there was real work to be done at the operational level. Lizzy took all of that off my plate. She sheltered me from most of the bull crap.

Designer Suit

Despite all the firing I was forced to do, the board still wanted me to allow a series of hires I came to loathe called the "3 Es": experienced, expensive, and executive. One costly hire in particular, Sybil, was chosen by the board to take on the role of president of Lolly Wolly Doodle. I was asked by some of our investors to step out of the way and let her lead the company. The board wanted a more experienced retail executive to "turn things around."

Sybil, or S.S., as she called herself, came with a pedigree. She was an Ivy Leaguer with an MBA who had been cred-ited with building a large department chain's e-commerce channel into a $500 million business.

Right away, she made it clear to everyone in our New York office that she was the boss. Angad and his team, like most techies, tended to be casual. They worked hard but irregular hours, sometimes remotely. It wasn't a nine-to-five workplace culture, and S.S., who'd stopped by for an informal chat a few days before her official start date, made a dig, warning them that things were going to change around there.

"It was off-putting," Angad told me later. "It wasn't even her first day; she didn't know us yet."

Sybil made a point of having lunch with Angad once a month to check in with him. She didn't fully understand what he was doing for us, but she did generously offer to help "groom" him to become what she believed would a better manager, like her. She demanded a lot of formal internal meetings with staff and insisted on creating a traditional corporate hierarchy. The rest of the time her office door was closed. People felt guarded and uncomfortable around her.

S.S.'s visits to Lexington were equally fraught. In the South we have a saying about people we are not terribly fond of: "Bless her heart." We blessed Sybil quite a bit. Poor Katie had to handle all of the special requests, making sure she could get gluten-free meals, a personal trainer, and a suite at the most expensive hotel in the area, which was about a thirty-minute drive away. One lunchtime, when we had food delivered, no one was around to answer the door. S.S. wasn't pleased when she had to get up and open it herself.

"What is the world coming to?" she asked. "I used to have my lobster served to me on a tray by my assistant."

Grumpy, Jackie, and all the other ladies on the factory floor were puzzled by this slick New York fashion executive dressed in head-to-toe Prada who breezed through the building with barely a glance in their direction. This time it really was the Sigourney Weaver character from *Working Girl*.

Culture Clash

The folks at the Doodle had grown used to seeing people from all walks of life turn up at the factory. As a little girl I used to dream about visiting exotic places and seeing the world, but the world was actually coming to Lexington.

Since that first order from China, I'd done some research and found a manufacturer there who could produce high-quality cotton goods that matched our standards. We would mass-produce these basic, evergreen items, or blanks, then customize them in our factory at home, adding a trim here, an applique there, so even Made in China got the Made in America touch. This was a factory in Zhejiang, an eastern coastal province of China, just south of Shanghai. Of course they made a few mistakes, which is bound to happen when you outsource to another country. But they always stood behind their work, either by crediting us for the next order or by swiftly redoing the production run if necessary.

We dealt with the factory manager, a sweet young woman barely out of school named Maggie Lin. She was the only one who spoke English. Maggie and I became friends over Skype, so we decided to invite her and the factory owner to Lexington to get a tour of our operation and familiarize themselves with our manufacturing process.

She was so excited to be in Lexington. She just couldn't stop smiling, touching my face, saying to everyone, "My best friend, my best friend!" Maggie and her boss insisted on taking pictures of themselves shaking everyone's hand. Her boss, the factory owner, couldn't stop grinning, and neither could

I when I saw the logo of his bright yellow polo shirt, which said "COCK" in big bold letters—obviously a local Chinese brand. I am sure he had no idea what it meant.

Maggie wept tears of joy when we took her to the local Walmart, where she stocked up on huge bottles of vitamins. They'd never seen so much volume and selection. When it was time to leave, Maggie cried again.

Gritty Charm

Redneck or not, we Southerners are generally a polite bunch. We want everyone to feel welcome. We feel proud when visitors from up North appreciate our fine barbecue, or the rolling hills and lakes of our countryside, or the quirkiness of our local characters and culture. When a stranger comes to town, my mother-in-law, Nana Faye, is only too happy to invite them over for some homemade cheesy hash brown casserole and the fluffiest coconut cake you ever tasted. You better come hungry.

Of course we have our moments, and the occasional culture clash is inevitable. Even Lizzy and I have had our misunderstandings. She disagreed strongly about a new phone system we were installing, and I didn't mind either way, so I said, "Okay, it is what it is." She took that to mean what I say goes, so for two weeks she was downright curt toward me. Finally, I asked her what was up and she explained how hurt she was. When I told her what I actually meant, that I was happy to go with whatever she decided, we both laughed. It was just a difference in dialect. To this day, when one of us uses that expression in front of the other, we bust out in giggles.

You can find common ground with anyone if you just try. As Angad got to know people in the North Carolina office better, he joked that being in the rural South was just like being in India, where it's all about family drama and everyone knows each other's business. He's made a lot of friends down here and seems to really enjoy his visits. He's been like a brother to me, and everyone at Lolly Wolly Doodle, from the sewing department to the warehouse, has embraced him as one of their own.

It's true there can be a lot of prejudice in a part of the country where folks don't often venture outside their 200-to-300-mile radius. Southerners can be some of the most narrow-minded people, because they live in a bubble where the only information they get beyond their county lines comes from television. They assume it's a crazy world out there and never get to experience it directly. But in many ways I think regular people around here are more open-hearted. They're quick with a smile and a "Hi, how y'all doin'?" and genuinely curious to know the answer.

There might be a few hot topics you'd want to stay away from, but it always bothered me that our colleagues in the New York office couldn't grasp that someone from Lexington could actually be intelligent. *As the saying goes, "When you assume you make an ass out of you and me." Some of the most traveled, educated, and experienced people I have ever met are more closed-minded than any of these Deep Southern people ever will be.*

Soon after S.S. took over, a parade of experts marched

through, each one rushing to judgment with suggestions that were more like mandates. She spent millions of investor dollars building up her executive team in New York and hiring an army of high-priced consultants who made no attempt to understand our business. Some were perfectly polite and respectful, and a handful were incredibly supportive and insightful, but many were openly contemptuous. Our gritty charm left them cold, and we detected more than one eye roll as they toured the manufacturing operations. It was obvious they wanted to be somewhere else.

It was frustrating to watch as they drew their conclusions without ever bothering to understand who we were or why we did things a certain way. They judged strictly on paper, sneering behind Amy's back because they couldn't understand how a nurse could possibly be qualified to design children's clothes. They questioned why Jordan, a former teacher, was in the tech department, but when I tried to explain the incredible job she was doing liaising between Angad and our entire sales and production team, they had already made up their minds. It didn't occur to them that people without all the conventional degrees and qualifications could learn and grow. We would have had to pay a fortune to bring out someone with Jordan's skill set to Lexington, with no guarantee that they would do the job half as well. These out-of-town experts had no concept of the complexity of their roles and could not have cared less that these people willingly worked overtime and weekends, treating this company as if it were their own.

This New York crew might have been huge assets to the large and more corporate retail companies they came from, but they created a lot of havoc with the culture I was trying to build at the Doodle. Whenever I interviewed a potential member of our executive team in Lexington, I'd say, "Okay, you might be a vice president of finance, a CTO or a CFO, but I am going to value you the same way I value a finisher in the factory."

I expected everyone to jump in and do whatever was needed. In no way was it acceptable to treat another employee as inferior or to make others feel less important somehow. I can't stand it when someone is belittled. Mammaw Betty always said, *"Everyone's shit stinks."* We were all shoulder to shoulder and willing to wear any hat if it was for the good of the Doodle. Randy, our controller, was right on the floor with us, pressing fabric prints to meet our Easter shipping deadline.

Then it became "us versus them." The atmosphere turned toxic overnight, like we were fighting the Civil War all over again. As they tend to do when the numbers are going in the wrong direction, the board was constantly questioning our process, even though our innovative approach was what had attracted them to us in the first place. Was it perfect? Of course not. We were growing and evolving, which meant we had to be in a constant state of tweaking. But that didn't mean we needed to become something completely different.

One of the consultants had worked with some of the biggest manufacturers in the United States. Early on I gave him a tour of the factory, and he was appalled by our cutting methods.

"Okay, either you have re-created the wheel, or what you are doing will never work," he told us.

Because we did limited-batch, customized, just-in-time manufacturing, we found it easier to work with more adaptable, single-paper patterns. Just-in-time production means we produce only the amount needed to meet customer demand, nothing in advance and with minimal surplus. It saves on costs because we receive goods like fabric and trims only as they are needed in the production process, thus decreasing waste and inventory costs. But this gentleman insisted we do what everyone else in the fashion industry does and use the Gerber system, in which computer-aided design technology is used to lay the fabric out and laser-cut larger quantities. I respected his opinion, because he certainly had the experience, and I wanted to hear what he had to say. But his overall argument that we needed to change out the entire system and his warnings that we wouldn't have accurate enough patterns if we used paper made no sense to me. For the kind of volume we did on each design pod, it would have taken three times as long to complete a production run. His logic applied to the traditional business model, not ours. After several months of back and forth, I was getting pressure from the board to switch to the Gerber system entirely, but I still wasn't convinced. I tested his theory with a small production run, just to make sure. The results spoke for themselves.

"You know what, you're right," he told me. "You have figured out a solution to just-in-time manufacturing that no one else has thought of. There may be a few hiccups, but your way is much better. Textbooks are going to be written about you."

Even if you disagree with someone, it's an opportunity to learn. Stand your ground, but listen carefully, even if you know from the beginning that they are wrong. Throughout our conversations, I was picking up tidbits here and there, little takeaways I could use. There is value in knowing the industry standard, even if it just bolsters your confidence in veering from what everyone else thinks is the right way.

But continue to question everything. No one knows your business as well as you do. I had accepted too many decisions by the investors and experts, to the point where we were top heavy with executives who knew how to do Power-Point presentations and not much else. As your company's founder, you have every right to quiz someone on what it is exactly they are going to do for you. Don't take anyone else's word for it.

The Trouble with Experts

As Mark Twain once quipped, "An expert is anyone out of town." That's what we were experiencing. To be clear, there's nothing wrong with seeking an outside opinion. When your business is growing faster than you could possibly imagine, it could benefit from a seasoned expert who has "been there, don't that," and can offer some helpful insight. But, *whether you are inventing something completely new, creating a revolutionary business model, or merely ruffling the status quo, an expert from the traditional trenches may not be the perfect fit for an entrepreneurial company like yours.* You need someone who is as entrepreneurial in mind-set as you are and willing to help you build the business that *you* want to build. Those kinds of experts aren't so easy to find.

To avoid making costly mistakes, **don't start with the title**. Old-fashioned job titles can send you down a rabbit hole of false expectations. Even if you think you need a vice president of operations, think of the top three objectives you want accomplished by the person sitting in that job. Be as specific as possible.

Of course, you need to know exactly what you need to start with. The best way to understand the top three objectives for the position that you are hiring for is to **do the job yourself**. Figure out exactly the gaps are in your own knowledge, experience, or bandwidth (you can't do everything). Chances are, you won't be able to fill the role perfectly, but you will quickly learn what skills you are seeking. Filling gaps in knowledge is the whole point of working with an expert, after all.

Get granular in your questions. If you're interviewing a job candidate from a traditional, top-down company, dig deep to find the specifics of his or her experience. Start-ups need someone who is hands on and flexible, and who has been close enough to the ground to understand that it's not just about managing people and developing processes. They have to be willing to roll up their sleeves and do it themselves. If you are looking for ERP experts, ask how many systems they've implemented, what the bugs were, how they were fixed, and what their specific role was. Don't discount someone if they come from a different industry. You might find their experience dovetails nicely with your needs, but you will never know unless you push for more details.

Never compromise or second-guess yourself. It's all too easy to be dazzled by the promise of experience, but tread carefully. Sure, in the beginning you could describe my hiring criteria as loose, but I was hiring at a whole different level, looking for passion and a willingness to learn and grow alongside a company that was in its infancy. When you are hiring at the expert level, however, a wrong hire can be an expensive mistake, in time, money, and business progress. *Make sure the cultural fit is right. If you are gutsy and fast-paced, more inclined to take smart risks, your expert has to share your vision, whether they come from corporate America or the start-up in the office next door.*

Look, you may think you don't measure up to their fancy business pedigrees. *Maybe you didn't finish college like me. Maybe you didn't finish high school. But if you're in a position to hire experts—look how far you've come!* You own a business. You've created a solution to a problem—a product or a service everybody wants—that no one else has thought of, not even the most brilliant business school graduates, and now they want to work for *you*. I don't care how many degrees or titles someone has.

The Straightjacket

My biggest mistake was meekly accepting these outside hires at face value because our investors, who weren't working with us day to day and couldn't possibly have understood our needs, told me to. I backed down too much and too quickly after the Facebook fiasco. I knew I'd fumbled. But that didn't discount all of the things we were doing right before circumstances changed. You don't fix what isn't broken. We were a start-up that was innovating. We were doing so many things that had never been done before, and we needed people who either thought just as much outside of the box or had the spirit to acknowledge and appreciate our level of innovation.

Instead, Sybil and her team of experts ended up straightjacketing Lolly Wolly Doodle into a traditional retail company, simplifying the list of product offerings and sourcing more product overseas. They wanted fewer custom offerings and more mass-produced items, shifting the balance of production from 50/50 overseas and Lexington to 80 percent produced offshore, mostly China, and 20 percent back home.

They were bowing to the latest trend in mass retail, which was cotton items. But because we were customizing less, our product lineup just wasn't that cute or special. Business was shrinking so much that we were attracting a discount customer. And yet members of the executive team insisted on increasing prices. All of a sudden a twenty-nine dollar dress cost forty-four, a fifteen-dollar price hike that our customer base noticed and resented. Our customers had much less to choose from and a much higher price point, so they voted with their feet. We ended up with a huge sale section on our website and way too much unsold inventory, a situation we never had to contend with before.

What these executives failed to grasp was that when you have a factory you have a certain amount of overhead. Our efficiency came from numbers. We could not afford to shrink our offerings. You can only cut your seamstresses' hours short so many days before you start losing them. We lost half of our sewers because there wasn't enough volume coming in. It was heartbreaking to watch all these seamstresses sitting idle. I could see the fear and frustration in their eyes. Well, I also heard it. People would come up to me daily with concerns that the Doodle was in trouble. I had to be diplomatic, but in my heart I agreed with everything my North Carolina Doodle team was saying. They knew that another round of layoffs was inevitable. There was even talk of closing down the factory and moving everything to New York.

I wasn't surprised. In the beginning S.S. would fly down from New York for three days a week. That whittled down to one day a week, then every other week. There wasn't much point to her being on the premises anyway, as she always shut her office door. The only time she really interacted with anyone else was when she giving her "President's Update." Everyone at the company had to stop what they were doing, gather around, and listen to her presentation, in which she invariably rolled out some statistic that was supposed to demonstrate how well we were doing and how bright the future looked. Of course no one believed her. Especially when there were more brutal layoffs the very next day.

That second round of cuts was especially gut wrenching because it was entirely preventable. Our investors had appointed these top executives, paying them high salaries in the genuine belief that they could turn things around. It wasn't the result they'd intended, but the jobs of honest, down-to-earth, working people were sacrificed to pay for this beefed-up management team. Members of our Lolly Wolly Doodle were facing financial ruin if they lost their next paycheck.

The board genuinely believed in what it was doing, but I was appalled by the waste and heartsick by the layoffs, most of which would not otherwise have been necessary.

Patrick and other family members were named on S.S.'s list of still further cuts. These were not redundant positions. For every person she had on her layoff list, I'd have had to immediately turn around and hire and train someone, and likely for more money.

Wes Turner, our warehouse manager, who'd left a high-paid job and moved his whole life to Lexington to take the job, was so disgusted with what was happening that he resigned with no backup plan. He made the sacrifice in the hope that the savings on his salary would allow four or five of the workers to stay in their jobs. The day he left was like losing another family member. This past Mother's Day, he sent me a message that touched my heart:

"Last year was one of the hardest of my life. But my LWD family was there for me and still is today. People seem surprised at my actions and choice when I left. But I think back to the moment when we were in your office, both crying, and I knew in my heart that my love for your family and what you stood for didn't leave me a choice. I believe when a man has a choice of right and wrong, it isn't even a choice. You only do what is right. So thank-you for being a great mother and source of inspiration, and impacting my life in a positive way!"

That message from Wes was a reminder of what this business means to the Doodlers who put everything on the line to see us succeed. They deserved so much better than the treatment they were getting from the New York office, which saw them as nothing more than a head count. By then we were down to ninety people.

When Sybil started making noises about closing down the North Carolina factory, I'd had enough. My brother Donnie happened to catch me one day when I'd reached the boiling point. There was really no one else I could unload onto, because I was still trying to abide by Lizzy's golden rule of sticking to the chain of command. Now, I'm not one to cuss, but this time I couldn't help myself. I turned the air blue as I raged on about S.S. and her New York posse. About halfway through I remembered that Donnie was now a man of God. He got saved a few years back and had joined one of those fire-and-brimstone Baptist churches where you don't drink, you don't swear, and you sure don't take the Lord's name in vain, not that my brother judges anyone.

"Oh my gosh, Donnie, I'm so sorry," I said, once I'd run out of cusses. But he just stood there smiling.

"That's okay, sis. Jesus is standing behind me and he doesn't mind."

That was my wake-up call. God was watching me, and I wasn't alone in this. Instead of bitching about it, I had the choice to actually get up and do something to stop the madness. God had blessed me with a business that had transformed so many lives around me, including my own. I had to do all I could to protect this gift. It was time for action.

AH-HA'S

- Avoiding the unpleasantness, hurt feelings, and guilt of laying people off risks killing the business. Kindness in the short term can be selfish and negligent in the long term, because by then everyone is out of a job.
- Don't make assumptions. You can find common ground with anyone if you just try.
- Everyone is equal, despite their title or salary. In no way is it acceptable to treat another employee as inferior or to make others feel less important somehow.
- Even if you disagree with someone, it's an opportunity to learn. Stand your ground, but listen carefully, even if you know from the beginning that they are wrong. You can always pick up tidbits here and there, little takeaways that matter.
- But continue to question everything. No one knows your business as well as you do.
- Be wary of experts. Whether you are inventing something completely new, creating a revolutionary business model or merely ruffling the status quo, an expert from the traditional trenches may not be the perfect fit for a company like yours.
- Seek someone who is as entrepreneurial in mind-set as you are and willing to help you build the business that you want to build.

- Don't start with the title. Old-fashioned job titles can send you down a rabbit hole of false expectations.
- The best way to understand the top three objectives for the position that you are hiring for is to do the job yourself.
- Get granular in your questions. Dig into the specifics of what this person can do for you and how he or she can apply their experience and skill set to their role in your company.
- Make sure the cultural fit is right. While it's possible to learn great lessons from someone with a different background, they must still share your values and work ethic.
- Don't be intimidated by fancy degrees or corporate pedigrees. If you're in a position to hire experts, look how far you've come!

Seven

Prepare for Battle

I respect a person that has had to fight and howl for his decency.

–Tennessee Williams

y room at the W Hotel in New York City's Union Square was starting to look like a war bunker. I usually went for something more low budget, but this might be the last time I could expense a business trip, and that spa-like scent of eucalyptus that hit me whenever I walked into the W's lobby always had such a calming effect that for once I decided to splurge. Not that aromatherapy could compete with the smell of fear. I had three days to prepare for a board meeting that would determine the fate of the company I had built, and I had knot upon knot in my stomach. I had to make the case for doing it my way or hand the keys over to Sybil, which I believed could lead the Doodle to die a slow and painful death.

New York hotel rooms are notoriously small, and there

were four of us squeezed into what became a kind of rival New York headquarters: me, Angad, plus two members of the New York team—one woman from accounting and another from merchandising—who said they believed in what we were doing and wanted to help. There we were, the outcasts, two on the little loveseat sofa, one at the desk, and me on the bed, with the rest of the floor space stacked high with reports. (When investors are involved, you wouldn't believe how much paper a company can generate over two years—we almost needed a second room.)

Except for a nice expensed dinner with a glass of good wine at the end of each long day, we holed up in there, living on room snacks and takeout. But there wasn't much camaraderie. All day long we fought with one another as we crunched the numbers and hammered out the best way forward. Everything we promised in that deck had to be realistic. Angad was a stickler on this point, and so was I. I wanted to be able to back up every single one of my statements with nothing but the facts—real metrics that told the story and could not be spun with sophisticated corporate jargon. It had to pass the truth test, because even though we figured we were almost sure to lose, I wanted to be able to stand behind every word.

"Oh, just BS them," said the woman from accounting during an especially heated argument. "We're not going to win anyway."

As much as I wanted to throw her out of the room, I had to remind myself that she didn't know what it was like to see lightning strike. She didn't get that you don't tempt fate, because she'd never seen fate get the upper hand. Life for her had unfolded in a predictable straight line, so she didn't realize that a 99 percent chance of failure also meant a 1 percent chance of victory. It wasn't much, but at least *we had a chance*.

Besides, I'm an old-school Southerner who believes in the honor of a handshake. I wasn't going to change my ways and start playing that game. I wasn't going to walk into that boardroom saying something I didn't totally believe in. Not now.

Numbers Don't Lie

I'd already been beating that truth drum with the investors for months, desperately trying to get them to see the reality of Lolly Wolly Doodle's decline. (Shana had resigned from the board when S.S. was hired, so I was on my own.) S.S. had a talent for putting a rosy spin on things in jargon that could impress anyone if they didn't bother to do the math. Surprisingly, given the millions of dollars she was spending, no one had dug deeply enough into the numbers, so I decided to do it myself.

Over the years I'd gotten pretty familiar with figures and stats. I could create an Excel spreadsheet as well as the next person. I could spot inconsistencies and trends, and when I looked closely at the real numbers it told me quite a story. We were circling the drain.

Several weeks before that hotel stay in New York, I called one of the investors to sound the alarm. To get his attention, I put together a report, complete with a breakdown of revenues, which, for the months January through July, had dropped $1.5 million. That wasn't because of Facebook. By then we had recovered and adapted our social media model. **When you're going against someone, get into the numbers and cold, hard facts. Never give them the chance to dismiss what you are saying as biased or personal.** I broke down sales by all of our different sales channels, from social media to our website and app.

I pointed out how S.S. and her team had taken over every aspect of the business that affects sales, from pricing structure and merchandizing, but wasn't being held responsible for the sharp drop in sales. She had authority but no accountability. I included customer surveys, stats on return rates, customer acquisition (and loss), and system-generated numbers to highlight the fact that the board was being given fuzzy data. I also talked about the fact that we were making up lost ground with renewed marketing and social media efforts. I listed all the ways the company was being derailed, from the misallocation of resources to the demoralization of our team with put-downs and micromanagement.

"This is no longer my vision," I wrote in my report. "I respect that I won't always know the best way to proceed; . . . however, I know the DNA of the company and that is disappearing fast. . . . I cannot work alongside individuals who see no value in my vision, our product, and do not understand or strive for innovation. . . . I understand that we are only as good as our team, and right now we are NOT a team. We have brought in some amazing execs with the ability to lead us forward, but the toxicity of only a couple of people will stall us and then completely stop us from any further progress. . . .

"I realize that I fumbled the ball before, I openly acknowledge that and accept responsibility. Our entire business changed almost overnight, and at the end of the day, I don't know of many businesses that survive that at all. However, the first time was on me, but this time it is on the board's shoulders. I have stayed out of the way, allowed S.S. to operate the business and build the team the way she felt most appropriate to grow the business, and we have instead declined by leaps and bounds. This is NOT my fumble!"

As soon as one of the investors saw my report, I heard back. He was anxious to talk and insisted on getting S.S. and me on a three-way conference call. Oh, she could talk, but I had the facts in black and white and countered every argument with the cold, hard truth: If we continued on this path, LWD would no longer exist. Around and around we went. It went on for days, and I was getting tired of repeating myself. Those endless calls and e-mails were toxic.

Stacked Deck

Meanwhile, as I was digging through all the memos and correspondence of the past several months to find a particular e-mail that I needed for my research, I logged into our gmail administrator account. When I typed in the name of one of our investors to look up the date of that message, all the e-mails ever sent to or from or about that person within the company e-mail system came up, at least as far as the subject line. I had the legal right to access everyone's company account, although I would never dream of looking at their private messages. Nevertheless, I stumbled upon the subject line of an e-mail from S.S. to her husband, referring to our upcoming meeting.

"OMG, did you see that note? I can't believe this nonsense. Guess this has now become a cage match. . . ."

As I continued to search I came across more revealing e-mail threads.

"Thinking of you this morning," a member of our board wrote to S.S. in one subject line. "Are we still talking at 2 today?" S.S. responded.

That's when I knew for certain the deck was stacked. I was tired and convinced that nothing I could do or say would sway the people in charge, despite all of the factual information I threw at them. I finally got another one of the board members on a two-way call and told him I was ready to resign.

"I am sorry but I can't go on like this. I think I am done. What are my options?"

"Whoa, wait! You can't resign!" he said, sounding genuinely shocked it had come to this. "Come to my office. The three of us will meet in person, and we'll go over the numbers line by line."

The meeting was hellish. At this point, S.S. and I couldn't stand each other. But I was willing to give it one last try, so I made him an offer.

"Listen, I'll continue to work with S.S., but she has to turn back over part of the operations to me, including design and marketing."

"Absolutely not!" Sybil replied, telling the investor to make a decision then and there. "Either she goes or I go," she told him.

The Fight of My Life

"Okay, this is how it's going to go. There is going to be an emergency board meeting," the investor told us later, in an e-mail. "I want the two of you to meet in front of the rest of the board members next week in New York. I want each of you to put together a twelve-month plan to present to everyone. At the end of the meeting, the board will vote. If Sybil is more convincing, she will be promoted to CEO and be put 100 percent in power. Brandi will be the chair and face of the brand. She will do all of the PR. If Brandi's case is more convincing, Sybil will be let go with a generous severance package, and Brandi will take over."

It was on.

With just a few days to prepare for the fight of my life, I was up day and night, digging through reports, memos, and e-mails. I wanted to demonstrate in no uncertain terms how, if we focused on technology and design innovation, kept to our core values, and allocated enough resources to our strengths, we could see tremendous growth within a matter of months.

I had never created a board deck from scratch before. That used to be Lizzy's department. I would say what I wanted in a presentation, but someone else would put it together. But this was the document to save the company. I had to oversee all of it this time. I had to 100 percent go for broke. But I wasn't alone. I had people helping me behind the scenes, including Angad, Amy, Jamie, and even a couple of the executives S.S. had hired. One by one, people were risking their jobs by coming to me with information that could help me bolster my case, letting me know what information Sybil had, and making sure I had access to all of the same reports, and then some. I sat down with Angad and our accounts people and went through the numbers line by line.

Forged Steel

Truth be told, those weeks leading up to our cage match, I was in a dark place of despair. I couldn't shut out a voice that was telling me that all of our efforts would be futile. This was a battle I did not expect to win. S.S. and her minions were going to be given free rein to run everything we had worked so hard to build right into the ground. I was already formulating a plan B. If I had to hand the Doodle over to someone else, there was no way I was going to stay and be a just a figurehead. Are you kidding me? Instead, I would hit reset with a brand-new company. I'd already carefully reviewed all of my contracts with my attorneys to figure out what my legal options were. I would be able take my best people with me, the folks S.S. did not appreciate and would immediately fire anyway, and together we would build something great with the business model I had envisioned all along. If we had to go back to my garage again, so be it.

The thought of losing this business built on love filled me with sadness. But then I flashed back to my greatest challenge, when Fran was suddenly and tragically taken from me.

My life with Frannie was a nonstop party. He was so magnetic and full of life people were drawn to him. I don't like sports, but I loved socializing and going to the games with him. Our life together was like an endless vacation. I didn't work. I just took care of Fran, Vivi, and Kade, although we had a nanny. I was Fran's baby mama, and that was fine with me. He made every moment of his life count, and it was just such an honor to be with him.

The night he died, he met friends for dinner and drinks while I stayed home with a girlfriend and looked after Vivi. (Kade was with his father in North Carolina for the week.) That Tuesday afternoon, as he was getting ready to leave, we bantered back and forth about what time he was coming home, and I can still picture him cracking wise behind the living room bar like it was yesterday.

"Maybe I'll come home, maybe I won't!"

"Oh, well, then maybe I won't be here when you do get your ass back home!" I joked back.

He had me and my girlfriend in hysterics, picking at us and joking about who he might meet that night. We were howling with laughter. Typical Fran had to get in one last zinger as he walked out the door.

"See ya later!" he said, then popped his head back in with a grin. "Or not!"

Later that afternoon Vivi and I had gone to the mall to pick out some outfits for a formal function we had to attend that Friday. We modeled the clothes we were trying on and texted them to Fran for his approval. When we got back we put on a movie, *Batman*. Viv always loved watching it with her daddy, who told her how he was going to knock out the Joker.

"When's Daddy coming home?" she asked me.

It was getting late, and it occurred to me I hadn't heard from him in a while.

That ass, I thought. *So typical of him to get caught up in the fun and forget to call.*

It turned out that he was coming home exactly when he promised. He'd died at 9 p.m. When the police came to our door in the middle of the night, I found out it had taken them so long to notify me because they'd seen Viv's car seat and a pair of her shoes in the back and thought she must have been in the car. They'd spent all that time searching the area expecting to find a baby thrown from the vehicle.

Fran's blood alcohol level was slightly over the legal limit, but I don't think that caused the accident. It had been raining hard and the road was slick, causing him to hydroplane and hit a mile marker. The collision happened at just the right spot to cause his car to flip over and over again. He was a stickler for wearing a seatbelt, but for some reason he didn't have his on that night. His body had gone through the sunroof and was momentarily trapped, so the car rolled on him. But when I saw his body at the morgue he looked good. There was barely a scratch on him, and no broken bones. The man was built like Shrek, but the strain of the impact tore his aorta, and he bled out instantly.

People wouldn't recognize the person I was before I lost Fran. I hardly ever cried. I was almost cold. I wasn't the mean girl, because I always had a soft spot for the underdog, but my friends gave me a bumper sticker for my sixteenth birthday that read, "World's Biggest Bitch," and it sure stuck. Then I lost my Frannie and I was a huge ball of mush. I get so emotional now. Even a television commercial can set me off. It's as if this loss pulled me wide open to a new way of thinking about life.

There's an art to losing. When the person you love the most is ripped away from you like that, it teaches you something. Fran was my everything, and when he was killed the floor got smashed out from under me. I was a weeping, wailing mess. But two people were put on my path who helped lift me out of the darkest depths of my grief. A long-lost friend of mine from Lexington had just moved to Orlando, and since I last saw her she had developed a relationship with God. She wasn't preaching. She wasn't out to convert me. It was more about loving God than going to church. But she would talk about her faith in a way that made me curious. Viv's nanny, Haley, was also deeply religious and talked about God all the time, but in a way that felt natural. When Fran passed she prayed for us and shared passages from the Bible to bring us comfort. The day after he died she wrote a song that she sang at the funeral to help us heal. It did.

We weren't a family that went to church regularly. Other than attending the odd service for Christmas and Easter, I didn't think about it much. But these two ladies inspired me. I was a woman on the brink, with nothing. I'd never felt more alone, so I turned to God and started praying these crazy fanatical prayers.

"Jesus, please, show me why this happened," I told Him. "That man was the center of my world outside of my kids. Give me a reason to wake up in the morning. People tell me you can be my husband, my best friend, my provider.... Show me!"

All that hard praying and crying suddenly ceased. I felt this overwhelming peace and comfort. I still wondered why, and ached for my Fran, but I surrendered and gave it all to God. Acceptance and understanding that it was in His hands got me through each day.

That was the point in my life when I first started to see how things came full circle. He knew He had to put some people in front of me who weren't going to shove their faith down my throat or tell me I was going to hell if I didn't accept Jesus as my Lord and Savior. It was an awakening gently nudged along by two caring women who happened to be in my life at a point when I needed them most. ***Albert Einstein once said, "A coincidence is God's way of staying anonymous." It wasn't random. Nothing ever is.***

Knowing there was someone so much bigger than me who had all of this in His hands took the pressure off me. ***I didn't feel like I had to figure it all out or know the answers. They would be revealed eventually.*** Those are the ah-ha moments when I say, "I see why You did that now. Wow, You are a genius!"

Facing off that overwhelming loss also helped me grow a stronger backbone. I was left alone with a baby and a young son from my first marriage, no job, not a dime to my name or a place to live. Looking back at that experience, I knew nothing could have been worse than what I already lived through, so if I lost LWD, so be it. No matter what the outcome, I would give it all I had and walk out of that meeting with my head held high. I'd already been fire tested, like forged steel, and coming through that loss was my secret superpower.

David and Goliath

That's what got me through those tense three days holed up at the W Hotel, preparing for the cage match—I mean, board meeting. That's why I kept trying, with all my heart, even when I was running on sleepless nights, fueled by leftover Chinese takeout.

When you find yourself pitted against someone powerful and the odds seem stacked against you, **don't give up before you have done all you can to make your case bulletproof.** I had to show, not tell, why my vision was better for the future of the company I had built, for everyone's sake.

Another big motivating factor was Angad, my other BFF. Like Lizzy, he is the one person who helps me keep it together emotionally. Somehow, even when he is in New York and I am in Lexington, he feels my stress. Countless times I will get a text from him saying, "What's up, are you okay?" and I'll wonder, *How the hell did you know I am freaking out?* From one crisis after another, he keeps our revenues going. He's the 911 operator, dispatching all the trucks and making sure nothing burns. He basically replaced Lizzy, and I've been so blessed to have him in my life. Since my Frannie died I've learned that when you lose someone, a new partner in crime could be right around the corner. You can even press reset and get another soul mate.

So I was fighting hard for Angad as much as for myself. He knew he couldn't stay at the Doodle if S.S. won this match. From the beginning, those two rubbed each other the wrong way. Angad was a Mac fan, so when S.S. bought a Surface tablet, she told him, "You probably won't be happy with me, but just remember before you react that I am your boss and I can fire you." It was probably meant to be a joke, but it was tone deaf, because Angad was here on a work visa. Losing his job would send him straight back to India.

He wasn't a yes-man, and he pushed back on several bad ideas, ultimately saving us a lot of money. Sybil outsourced all of our Facebook advertising to a big agency. It was unimaginative at best, because they used the same generic playbook for all of their clients, and it cost us a fortune with lousy results. Angad, who is a social media marketing genius, brought advertising in house, and the traffic on our page exploded. Under Sybil he took so many risks, putting the company before his own best interests.

Between the New York and North Carolina offices, the rumor mill was churning. Angad hadn't been into the official New York office for four days. He'd been taking the train in from his home in New Jersey every day to help me. At one point, he got wind of a plot to fire him if S.S. were to become CEO. It was a reminder of just how much was at stake not only for me but for him. For everyone. This time it was not just my dream and my family's income on the line; it was the fortunes of what was left of our entire Lolly Wolly Doodle family.

As we were preparing, my mother-in-law, Nana Faye, was busy making calls to the "prayer warriors"–the church ladies of Lexington, who prayed furiously for the future of the Doodle. We sure needed God on our side. We were still completing that thirty-page PowerPoint down to the wire. Angad wanted more numbers, more facts. He was afraid that I would be going into that meeting with something half baked. But by the end of that third day of preparation, I knew in my gut we had given it all we had. **When you lay your head on the pillow at night—or in my case the small hours of the morning—you just have to believe that you did everything you could. That's all God asks.**

The next morning, September 24, 2015, I was so scared I wanted to throw up. I took half a Valium, threw on a pair of jeans and a blazer (Banana Republic this time), and walked over to where the cage match was taking place, at one of our investors' offices on Fifth Avenue. On the way, the whole situation seemed surreal. On that crowded New York pavement, I was walking toward my fate. Everything we had worked for could be gone in one presentation.

The Cage Match

Once again, I found myself in the conference room of a glittering high-rise in Manhattan. To my utter amazement, the board had us in the room together for our presentations, sitting face to face in our fight to the finish. How awkward! Although I was relieved when they announced that S.S. would be going first.

According to her plan, we would have run out of money by July. She couched it all in lot of fancy words, but she couldn't hide the fact that it was a miserable fail. She wanted another $2 million from the board.

"I'm sorry, what?" one of the investors said. "I thought this was on the understanding that the last $6 million was it and you wouldn't be asking for more."

"But you guys said you would fund us as we continued to grow," Sybil replied.

Silence. By the looks on the board members' faces, they weren't buying any of it.

Then it was my turn. Half of my presentation was focused on exposing instances of waste and mismanagement within the business. As I flipped the sheets, I looked over to see S.S.'s expression, which was oddly blank. My heart was in my mouth as I launched into strategy. Not only did I project that we would be walking out of the year with money in the bank, I described exactly how we were going to get there. It was obvious that my vision would bring revenue growth and Sybil's plan would lead to losses. With five pages left to go, one of the investors raised his hand.

"Okay, I think we've heard enough."

They sent us into separate offices to wait while they took a vote and made the decision. To his great credit, Donn Davis had reached out to Shana and asked her to be present, to assure the neutrality of the board's decision. That gave me comfort. It was tense, but I felt proud of the job I'd done. I knew I left it all out on the floor. I texted Angad to let him know, and pinged my husband to tell him how it went.

All this time, Will was standing in the middle of the factory, which had come to a standstill. Unbeknownst to me, all but four people at the Doodle, from the senior management to the seamstresses, had signed a petition, letting the board know that if I wasn't put back in charge, they'd walk. These amazing people would rather have risked their livelihoods than stay with the company as it was.

After a few minutes, I heard them call in Sybil. I missed

her leaving the boardroom because I had to run into the ladies' room. I had no idea it would be so quick. Then they called me in.

"Brandi, we just wanted to let you know that the decision was unanimous," Donn said. "Sybil is leaving and you will be running the company as CEO."

Just like that. I didn't know whether to laugh or cry. A few hours before, I couldn't have imagined this outcome. I was convinced we would lose.

At first I had to stuff my emotions as I rode the crowded elevator three floors down to the lobby. My elation was so high, I could have been riding to the top of the Empire State Building as I discreetly texted and called everyone.

As I called Will to tell him the news, I was shaking.

"We won," I whispered into the phone, but the reception was bad.

"What was that honey? What happened? I can hardly hear you."

"The board saw in our favor. We're back in charge."

In the background, you could hear a pin drop. I listened as he belted out, "She won!" Then the whole factory erupted into cheers. Later on I saw the video: People were whooping, jumping, and hugging each other, tears of joy streaming down their faces. You couldn't have written a better movie scene.

Out through the lobby and into the noisy streets I joined them, whooping and shouting. I must have looked like a crazy woman, but I didn't care.

"Oh my gosh, I can't believe it's over. The Doodle is ours again. We did it!"

It just goes to show, you've got to keep the faith in your own vision. I had accepted the mandates of these investors because the money they gave made me feel I had to live by their expectations. I also lost confidence in myself after the Facebook bomb. I was too quick to cede control to individuals who I knew in my heart were wrong for us. I forgot the very reason these investors were attracted to my business in the first place, and so did they. But allowing them to do what I knew in my gut was wrong for the Doodle made it worse.

Not that I regret any of it. Not a thing! At the end of the day, the board's mandates gave us a fighting chance. At the rate we were headed, we wouldn't have survived before the investors stepped in. It allowed us to wake up and fight for our company. As frustrated as I had been with the board's decisions at the time, they forced us to pinch pennies and hold tight to our vision. It was a hard lesson to learn, and the immediate outcome wasn't what the board had intended, but the end result saved the company, and for that I am eternally thankful.

All those little failures along the way teach us something. The mistakes we make can turn into a reawakening. I hit the reset button on my confidence, took back control, and became a better leader. I rediscovered the inner strength I always had.

Just before the meeting, I posted something on Instagram. My design team, Jackie and Erica, saw it, reposted it, and within minutes it was trending. Everyone at the Doodle had adopted it as their new Facebook profile picture. When I got back, they had it written on T-shirts and a victory cake. They

printed out and pinned it to every wall in the building. It became our mantra:

*Be you and don't compromise. Do it unapologeti-
cally. Don't be discouraged by criticism or doubt. You
likely know the outcome, but pay no attention to the
fear of failure. Failure is far more valuable than success.
Take ownership and control. And no matter what, never
stop fighting for what you believe in. And have fun!*

AH-HA'S

- When you're going against someone, get into the numbers and cold, hard facts. Never give them the chance to dismiss what you are saying as biased or personal.
- There's an art to losing. We all experience devastating losses, but they teach us something.
- Albert Einstein once said, "A coincidence is God's way of staying anonymous." Nothing is ever random.
- Trust that the answers will be revealed eventually. Those are the ah-ha moments when I say, "I see why You did that now. Wow, You are a genius!"
- When you find yourself pitted against someone powerful and the odds seem stacked against you, don't give up before you have done all you can to make your case bulletproof.
- When you lay your head on the pillow at night, you just have to believe that you did everything you could. It's all God asks.
- Keep the faith in your own vision. Never hand over control wholesale or accept the mandates of third parties at face value. When you know in your heart something is wrong, speak up!

- All those little failures along the way teach us something. The mistakes we make can turn into a reawakening.
- Take ownership and control. And no matter what, never stop fighting for what you believe in. And have fun!

Eight

Expect the Unexpected

It's failure that gives you the proper perspective on success.

–ELLEN DeGENERES

I t was supposed to be a fresh start; another hit of the reset button.

Now in full control of the company I'd founded, I was ready to release a whole bunch of new designs that would expand our customer base and get the North Carolina factory humming again. We had a lot in our pipeline, but so many layoffs under the old regime put the business in a weakened position. We had lost some of our best seamstresses, and finding new skilled workers was an ongoing challenge. By the end of 2015 the local economy had picked up, and new furniture and textile factories were hiring. Now we had to compete with them to attract skilled workers. It was great for Lexington but a serious handicap for us. Just as we needed to pump up the volume, we were forced to make do and hire less-experienced sewers and train a large chunk of our workforce all over again.

But we felt confident. The atmosphere around the factory had transformed in a heartbeat. Folks were galvanized by the cage match victory and excited to help me rebuild the business. It was the morale boost we desperately needed. Everyone at the Doodle felt a pride of ownership and sense of vindication. It was like the early days, only better, because we were wiser. We'd been battle tested and won. Now we knew that we were on the right path.

And I had our launchpad—the design and printing capabilities to turn blank white fabric into one-of-a-kind fashion. It was the missing piece we needed to leverage our ERP technology and all its capabilities underneath. Now a customer could type in an order on our app or website and say, "I want my initials." A simple online feature enabled them to talk to our system, which would understand that the dress in size 10 needed to have the letters ABC or BLT printed within the design of the fabric. This wasn't embroidering a monogram separately, the monogram *was* the fabric. Now our customers had more options.

It was a departure from our previous design and manufacturing process, when we were able to grow quickly by using lots of unique printed fabric that we could buy fifteen yards at a time wholesale from our fabric suppliers. We'd make one or two items, and if they sold well, fine, we'd order more. If not, we'd sell what we had and quickly move onto something else. It enabled us to do fast iterations. But this new system, where we could design and print something fully custom, allowed us to respond even more quickly if we had a hit. And we could launch brand-new designs—items that did not exist anywhere else on the market, almost instantly.

Whatever we temporarily lacked in personnel we could make up for with this new technology. We streamlined the different machines we could use to make the factory more efficient as we continued to scale. But it would also help smooth out the work flow as we hit those seasonal surges in orders.

If you wait for the perfect moment to do something, it may never happen. We were as prepared as we could be for the next do-over. We had most of our infrastructure and just enough people in place to support our original vision of 100 percent mass customization. We had a strong legacy social media customer base to tap. Our technology was moving forward. We were getting back to our roots—creating, customizing for individual tastes and needs, and connecting with customers. We were poised for our big comeback and ready to make some history.

Legging-geddon

One of the first new products we offered with this technology was custom leggings. Shana, among our many other moms, had been pushing me to introduce leggings for the past year because of her daughter Arden, but it was one of many ideas I held back until the ownership and direction of the Doodle was clear. Now was the time. If it worked, it could bring back customers whose tweens and teenage daughters had outgrown the more cutesy, ruffled outfits that were our trademark. Leggings were versatile, age proof, and evergreen.

We gave our customers a choice of designs like medallions,

paisleys, even emojis. They could either order from our selection of ready-made styles or go on our website, choose
their color combinations, and enter their names or monograms, which would then be printed on the fabric, cut, and
stitched by our team of seamstresses.

We launched the first designs on January 24, which happened to coincide with our Easter sale. The website promised Easter delivery, but Easter came early that year. I expected
to sell up to 100 pairs of leggings a day. Because we had only
one printer, the timing of our production run had to be perfect. Down to every second of every day, we calculated how
many leggings we would have to print to ship before the
deadline. From the first day, sales were strong and we hit our
goals. By the second week, when we introduced our next
round of styles, sales started climbing fast: 100 a day, 200 a
day, 300 a day–it just kept going. Demand was overwhelming, and we were at running full capacity, all pistons pump-
ing. It was like those early Facebook blowup years all over
again. It was the big comeback in volume we needed–the
miracle we'd all prayed for. Until the machine broke down.

We'd been running that machine nonstop for months, and
it wasn't the first time it malfunctioned. But until this legging
run, repairs were usually quick and the setbacks were minor.
Apparently this time the problem was something the factory
that made the machines hadn't even seen before. It took the
company that serviced the machine until 4 p.m. the next day
to arrive, and they weren't able to repair it on the spot. Days
passed, then a week. They ordered a spare part that never
came.

We were repeatedly told that the machine would be fixed

within twenty-four hours, so at first we trusted that and kept selling. But orders were quadruple what we planned for, and I hadn't anticipated that our customers would be buying our leggings for Easter gifts and expecting that same delivery time. In my mind, they had been two separate groups of customers, but when everyone saw that we had leggings, they lost their minds. Everyone wanted a pair, or three. The problem was that we promised seven- to ten-day delivery all over our website, social media pages, and app. By then we'd changed the time frame to twenty-one days, but nobody who'd already placed an order noticed, and why would they? If I didn't do something fast, we were screwed!

We were running on fumes, doing round-the-clock shifts. Everyone from accounting to shipping was doing one thing: leggings. Family members pitched in; friends stopped by. We were in triage mode to get those leggings out.

I decided to buy two more of the machines as backup. Because we were such good clients, the machine distributor, who had printing capabilities at his facility, offered to pitch in and print some of our files. But about a third of what they printed turned out to be duplicate, another third never got printed, and we had no way of knowing because we weren't there. Everything that could possibly go wrong went wrong. Monograms were programmed in backward. A gallon of paint spilled on a new fabric order. The hot pink leggings came out orange. In the end, 5,000 leggings failed to get out on time.

The phone started ringing, and angry posts on social media screamed, "Where are my leggings?!" Customer service e-mails went from 100 a day to 1,000. It was freaking ridiculous. So many random things went wrong it was bizarre. The worst thing that could happen, happened, every single day. With thousands of angry customer e-mails to return and not enough hours in the day to fix every problem, I was hysterical.

"Lord, what do you want from me?" I asked, sitting in my little IKEA office chair, laughing like a maniac. "Is that all you got? Bring it on down! At least burn this place to the ground so I can get the insurance money!"

I was losing it. Nothing about the situation was funny, but all I could do was laugh.

Life's "Gotcha"

We burned a lot of the customers we'd been trying so hard to win back. In the end, only 100 true Easter items failed to make it out the door on time, which in the grand scheme of things could have been worse. About 2,500 were technically late, and we prioritized the orders with Easter motifs so that at least we wouldn't be responsible for ruining our moms' family holidays. But that wasn't the point. ***It would have been better to underpromise and overdeliver, because Murphy's Law always comes into play.***

That was another lesson God wanted me to learn. We'd been trying to build back the business, working on custom leggings and the technology behind them for months and months, and we thought we were ready. It would have been impossible to have anticipated all of those crazy mishaps, but we should never have cut it so close. If we had told those customers from the beginning that delivery time was twenty-one days, they would have been fine with it. In the custom clothing industry, customers are used to waiting three weeks or more, so they would have been pleasantly surprised. But we got a little too cocky with our new technology and broke a promise.

We all worked on e-mails for two weeks straight. By April 17 I was still personally answering e-mails dated March 17. We had a canned message about what happened, acknowledging the horrible customer service and offering refunds. But we felt the burn on social media. It was such a witch hunt that we had to go off the radar for the next six weeks and not release anything, holding back a new line of capris even though it was a key selling season for us.

When a miracle happens, be prepared for it. We badly needed a home run and we got one. We couldn't have imagined a better return on our investment. But the orders were almost too good to handle, and it nearly blew up in our faces. By then our early success on Facebook was a distant memory, and we had forgotten that anything is possible. *God provides, and when you pray for rain, get your ark ready because you might just end up with a flood.*

Of course, any entrepreneur will tell you to leave plenty of room for error. *But sometimes no matter how hard you prepare or how much leeway you give yourself, that perfect storm will hit, and all you can do is get through it.* There are times when you will never have enough backups. It's like when you bring that extra change of clothes and diapers for the baby. As soon as you get somewhere a diaper leaks and the mess gets everywhere. Then as soon as you change him your husband leans over and spills his drink. You've only gone out for a quick Sunday brunch, but it looks like you've packed for a week-long road trip, and you still don't have enough clean diapers.

Sometimes life just screams, "Gotcha!" And that's okay. You get back up, survive it anyway, and become more determined and prepared to get it right the next time, and the next. You hit reset again and again and again, and each time it gets a little bit, or a lot, better.

After our Facebook sales imploded, we did exactly that. We learned to envision not just a potential problem but the solution. ***When things go wrong and you make mistakes, or circumstances get out of control, it's not failure. It's experience. It's a chance to learn another lesson, even if that is something as simple as acceptance.***

There was no way we could have anticipated that the new printer would die. It had been running smoothly for eight months prior to Legging-geddon. Nor could we have predicted that our backup printing plan at the distributor's facility would complete only 60 percent of the orders. Based on past experience, there was nothing we could have done to prevent the malfunction or speed things up. It wasn't like having a computer that refused to turn on. We couldn't just buy another one at Best Buy, although I made the extra investments in the end. Those were expensive custom pieces of equipment that you couldn't just buy off the shelf. Most start-ups wouldn't be able to afford that kind of backup plan for a what-if scenario.

Like the clumsy fall that breaks an arm, it wasn't funny at

the time, but now we all laugh about it. Legging-geddon will go down in Doodle lore. It was an expensive practice run. But we learned beyond a shadow of a doubt that leggings were a tremendous blessing for us. Thank-you once again, Shana. You were right! There was all this pent-up demand, and what happened was God's way of saying, "See? You should have listened to her earlier. In your face!" It was another reminder that I am not always right. ***You think that you know the business like the back of your hand and you are the only authority, but other people can hit home runs for you.***

We fell a bit behind but not by much. And the ultimate takeaway was that we had a huge blockbuster on our hands. The legging fiasco, catastrophic as it was, turned out to be the ultimate proof of concept. It was part of a bold new mission for Lolly Wolly Doodle that would allow for more customization by our customers: Designed by You.

"YOU" Fashion

Personalization and customization was always the direction we needed to take, but we had been detoured while the old New York team focused on trying to turn us into a traditional retail company. All this time a few of us had been chipping away at designing the programs and app to make this possible on a mass scale, but we weren't getting the allocation of resources we needed. This was a big part of the cage match presentation that convinced our investors to go with my vision for the future. Finally, we were going to become the cutting-edge, twenty-first-century brand that would make "YOU" fashion a textbook term. Lolly Wolly Doodle had always been a socially driven fashion brand that turned shopping into a personal experience, but we needed to take it to the next level through technology.

The goal was to put the tool in the customer's hands. We wanted to empower both women and girls to make their own choices in what they wear. Of course we will always have a collection of our own designs and patterns, but more and more our moms and children want to stand out as individuals. As a country we are embracing differences more. We are teaching kids to express themselves and be their own person. Social media, and the way we tend to celebrate our children's uniqueness even more these days, has made this possible. Just look at the strides in gender roles that have happened in the past five years. It's okay for boys to play with baby dolls and wear a skirt if they want to. Showing the world who you truly are is no longer considered weird; it's an asset.

Adults and children alike want to be different. Again, people don't want to walk in and see themselves three times when they go somewhere. They're more like how I used to be in middle school, with my thirty-day rule. With our Designed by You feature, a little girl can go in and customize a pair of leggings if she wants to. I'd have loved something like this when I was a child! She might not have a single pattern that matches with stripes, polka dots, and smiley faces in any color combination, but it's all her creation. In my perfect world, a nice lady in the grocery store will stop her mother and ask, "Where did she get that?"

"Oh, it's this place called Lolly Wolly Doodle. She designed it herself."

The oddness of the little girl's design becomes its charm.

"Oh my Lord, isn't that adorable! What did you say was the name of that website?"

No one else in my industry was offering this capability to their customers, at least not at our level. It was how we intended to create our own unique section of the fashion marketplace, with customization features and an app that would give each customer the opportunity to personalize through every interaction with our brand, whether it was through targeted e-mail content based on user profiles and browsing history or more personalized landing pages. Customization was key to growing the business. It was a way to harness the power of the customer, learn what they liked and didn't like, help them make it their own, and constantly excite them with new things in a way that was still cost effective.

If this worked, the savings would be enormous, and we could pass that on to our customers. With the capability of designing and printing fabric in house, we could carry a huge supply of white fabric and waste little to none of it. Some of the biggest overhead in apparel manufacturing is the excess scraps. But now we had a system that could nest each piece precisely so that we could print and cut only what we needed, without having to commit.

For this reason, we also benefited from having less inventory. Larger apparel companies have to commit to 50,000 pieces. If they do something in coral and it doesn't sell, they are screwed. That's why it might cost $80 to begin with and then drop down to as low as $20. They have to discount the inventory unless they are an elite retailer, in which case they sell it offshore or burn it. But we never had that problem. With the exception of that period under the old New York regime, we introduced ours for $40, and our customer bought it for $40. When something didn't sell, they never saw it again. We could just take the item down the next week.

Of course, we would have to refine our process and hire people who could do more assembly-line work, focusing on elastic, for example. Instead of the limited-batch items cut and sewn using the short-order cook approach, we could scale up and do more mass production. Our technology could create the appearance that we were producing thousands of new units when in fact we were only customizing a handful of base items. It was a way to ease up on production costs and push up our gross margins.

Our customization approach also took care of the next wave of ankle biters. They'll always be there, which is flattering. But it's also annoying. We'd created the market and weathered the storms, and they came along to lap up the cream. Many from the first wave of imitators didn't survive when Facebook changed its algorithms, but we were beginning to see our look in the catalogues of CWDKids, Chasing Fireflies, and many other companies larger than ours. Creating our own fabrics put us several steps ahead of even the most established retailers. We could shake them off long before they had the chance to nip at our heels.

Bigger Footprint

Customized fabric would also allow us to expand our reach beyond the Southeast. Aesthetically speaking, so much of what had been doing was very Southern, with our largest customer base in Texas, Alabama, and the Carolinas, where they adore ruffles and bows. We wanted to make sure we didn't have as much exclusion as before. So if a customer in California saw a design template but didn't like something with all that extra detail, she could buy it without. We could continue to offer our unique range of styles and patterns, while customization and an expanded repertoire would give us an overall larger appeal.

And the greatest news of all was that we could keep most of our manufacturing in the States. Before this reset, more and more of our production had been moving off-shore. That wasn't true to my original vision. We took it back, and today I am proud to say that 75 percent of Lolly Wolly Doodle orders are produced back home in Lexington, North Carolina.

We still had so much runway. We'd already picked the lowest-hanging fruit, and now it was time to expand our thinking and give people more options. You have to constantly excite people with new things. We'd never had a large baby business, but the personalization technology allowed us to offer personalized baby gifts—for all the moms who were now becoming grandmothers.

Be true to yourself, but realize that a business is a living, breathing thing that needs to be nurtured in

order to be sustained. Your customers' lives and needs constantly change, especially when they have children. Lolly Wolly Doodle looks very different today than it did a few months ago. Although we have many of the same customers, their kids have grown, just as we have as a business.

And accept that you won't ever be able to hit cruise control. When you are running your own business, you will never have that moment to sit back, survey your empire, relax, and exhale. I wanted that sense of achievement so badly, but it never happened. From the moment I put that first smock dress up on Facebook, I've never stopped to catch my breath. As much as I'd love to be able to float, I've gotten so used to swimming upstream, I'm getting good at it.

The moment you tell yourself you've arrived, there will be some other challenge to face, but when you are an entrepreneur you will rise to it. It doesn't stop until you sell your company, and I'm not ready for that, yet. I'll know when God tells me, but it won't be in an e-mail or a Facebook post. The signs will be subtle. I'll have a decision to make, and the right one for me will bring a sense of peace.

So suck it up, buttercup. That's business. The movie version of my story would have ended on the high note of the cage match victory, but that's not how it works when you are an entrepreneur. *You can set up state-of-the-art systems, plan ahead, and hire great people, but at some point something is always going to go wrong. It's as true in business as it is in life, and that's okay, because each time it happens you get faster, smarter, and better.*

Every now and then, when I am feeling a little too satisfied with myself, God sends me these not-so-little reminders that He isn't done teaching me yet. But no matter how tough it gets, I have faith that His plan is greater than anything I could dream up myself, so I just keep going.

AH-HA'S

- Pull the trigger. If you wait for the perfect moment to do something, it may never happen.
- It's better to underpromise and overdeliver, because when you cut it close, it's like you are asking for something to go wrong. Never put yourself in that position.
- When a miracle happens, be prepared for it. God provides, and when you pray for rain you might just get a hurricane.
- There are times when you will never have enough backups. No matter how hard you prepare or how much leeway you give yourself, that perfect storm will hit, and all you can do is get through it.
- Sometimes life just screams, "Gotcha!" And that's okay. You get back up, survive it anyway, and become more determined and prepared to get it right the next time, and the next.
- When things go wrong and you make mistakes, or circumstances get out of control, it's not failure. It's experience. It's a chance to learn another lesson, even if that is something as simple as acceptance.
- You think that you know the business like the back of your hand and you are the only authority, but other people can hit home runs for you.
- Be true to yourself, but realize that a business is a

living, breathing thing that needs to be nurtured in order to be sustained. Your customers' lives and needs constantly change, especially when they have children.

- Accept that if you've chosen the path of an entrepreneur, you won't ever be able to hit cruise control. When you are running your own business, you will never have that moment to sit back, survey your empire, relax, and exhale.
- You can set up state-of-the-art systems, plan ahead, and hire great people, but at some point something is always going to go wrong. It's as true in business as it is in life, and that's okay, because each time it happens you get faster, smarter, and better. So suck it up, buttercup!

Nine

Spread the Blessings

You can't out-give God.

–2 CORINTHIANS 9

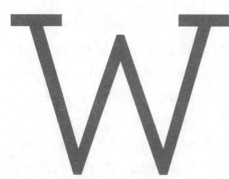hen people ask me if I would willingly put myself through this torture again, I immediately say no. But after a couple of beats I change my answer to *yes*. The reason? An ordinary-looking bottle of water, which sits in a place of honor on a shelf at our Lolly Wolly Doodle headquarters in North Carolina.

Its crystal-clear contents have traveled a long way, from a place I had never heard of, much less been to: a tiny, dust-blown village in Burkina Faso, a landlocked little country in northwest Africa.

Pete Brokopp, a gentle giant of a man who had been friends with my husband for many years, was a missionary who had devoted his life to taking God's love to the ends of the earth, and he and his family had been stationed there for many years. I had the privilege of meeting him when he was back in North Carolina on sabbatical. Pete described in detail to Will and me how more than 3 million people in that part of the world had no access to safe, clean drinking water. Children were getting sick unnecessarily from water-borne diseases. Little girls were getting raped as they walked to a river or some other source miles away, alone, to travel back to their huts laden with heavy jerry cans. The water shortage is an ongoing problem in that country. During the dry season, which lasts from March until June, it gets worse, with weeks-long power cuts and price hikes at pay fountains.

This just didn't sit right with me. Sure, there's poverty in our part of the world, but nothing like that. At least our poorest of the poor have access to running water and power. But these people were so lacking in the basics of survival that they were dying. So what could we do about it?

In 2012, Will and I decided that we wanted to bless others the way we had been blessed by funding a well to be drilled the following dry season. Pete was part of an organization whose mission was to bring clean water to the remotest areas, and the well project was put in motion. By coincidence, our church group was visiting that spot the day the well opened. They prayed over that first pump, distributed LWD T-shirts we had sent with them, and gave money for other supplies needed by the village. It was a small project, but it would impact the lives of hundreds of families who lived in the area. The water inside that plastic bottle comes from deep in the ground of that village.

When the mission members came to our headquarters to show everyone what they did, with pictures and a documentary, as well as notes from grateful children and families, there wasn't a dry eye on our factory floor. ***It's one thing to know what's going on in the big wide world in the abstract, but when you realize that you have done something that directly affects people's lives and you get so see their smiling faces after the fact, it touches your heart at the deepest level.*** Everyone in our LWD community felt a part of something larger than themselves. They'd had a hand in transforming hundreds of lives. And that's exactly why we're here.

For all of us, Lolly Wolly Doodle is about so much more than business. What was just a way to put food on the table for my family has grown into something much, much bigger than the small dreams and ambitions I started out with. It's given us a chance to make a positive difference in our community and the world. It's become a part of God's plan, and it's been incredibly humbling to look back and see all that we've accomplished as a team. We've been blessed. I've been blessed.

Torn to Pieces

But I've had my moments. I cannot lie. ***Anyone who starts, builds, and sustains a business and tries to tell you it's all a joyride is peddling BS. When you are a wife, a mother, and a boss, you never feel like you're doing enough.*** I'm treading water constantly, hoping not to drown. There are moments I feel torn into pieces as I try to juggle work and family. I don't know about other families, but I've found that you never truly switch roles even when your husband agrees to be the stay-at-home dad—at least that's not the case for my generation. Somehow he just ends up getting in more golf games. But a mom is a mom, and no matter how many other responsibilities she may have out in the world, nothing can replace the love and attention she gives to all the little details that matter at home. There are so many moments I have to decide between making the art show and launching a new line, taking a board call or opening the door to a worker who wants to talk about a serious personal problem.

A couple of years ago, I spoke at a CEO conference hosted by American Express, and somebody asked me how I balanced motherhood, family, and business.

"That's a great question," I told him. "If you figure out the answer, can you let me know?"

A woman came up to me afterward and said, "I am so sorry they asked you that question about being a mother."

"Oh, why?" I asked her, genuinely puzzled.

"They never would have asked a man that question."

I wasn't offended at all. It was a perfectly valid point. *As your business or career takes off and you find yourself wishing you could clone yourself, you will struggle to come up with an answer to the riddle of work/life balance.* I do, every single day. I even Google this question, like I do everything else I bump up against in life. I find stuff on how to be a better mom or how to ground your kids effectively. But there is nothing out there that tells you what to do when you feel like you are not giving enough to anyone or anything around you.

Sure, I could set more boundaries and learn to say no, but

the reality is that a CEO mom will always feel this way. *I don't care how much someone tells you to lean in. When you have children to care for, it's just part of the deal.* But how do I pick and choose? I don't want to miss a single thing with my kids, who have been amazing through all of this. They're old enough now that they can see what their mother is trying to do and appreciate the impact it is having on lives besides their own. Even though they get frustrated with me sometimes, they get it. They are bighearted Christians full of loving-kindness on their best days. They know I'm not doing this just to indulge myself.

But I still hate the fact that, during my son's baseball game, I have to sit on a hill and take a conference call from the board while watching him as he's up to bat. I miss very little if I am not out of town, but I don't want to be the mom who runs in to gives two hugs and three kisses and runs back out again.

And then there is my family at the Doodle.

The Circus Master

Not a week goes by when I don't wonder what the heck I signed up for. "Are you kidding me?!" "Seriously?!" How many times have you said or thought the exact same thing? I said it so often in the early years of the Doodle that my staff had a T-shirt printed up for me that read, "Seriously????!!!!" so that I could just point to it and save myself precious energy for putting out yet more fires.

Being an entrepreneur is nothing like the glamorous

vision we had when we first started, when money was pouring in from every corner and we were the darlings of the tech and retail world. I don't live a life of luxury, sitting behind a mahogany desk in a Chanel suit writing checks like Joy Mangano in the final scene of her biopic. I wish! I'm more like a circus master trying to remain calm and in control in the middle of three rings of total chaos.

The crazy ride starts in the clown car. One by one, these jokers keep climbing out as you watch wide eyed, trying to imagine how they can all fit in that tiny vehicle. That itty-bitty car they got out of? It's your budget, and those clowns are the employees and contractors you work with on a daily basis. Ever notice that none of them looks the same? It's because they aren't. They think and act differently, coming as they do from all backgrounds and walks of life, and you have to be sensitive to their needs as they exit. Some are skipping, some are pushing and shoving, some look like they could take you out right where you stand, and there is nothing you can do but throw your hands up in the air and laugh as you watch the show. The reality is that there is never enough room inside the clown car. You are constantly forced to work within tight constraints, whether they are financial or logistical, or your market share is closing in you while a never-ending stream of wannabe competitors tries to take a swipe. No wonder everyone has to squeeeeeeze!

One of the circus rings contains a daredevil on a motorcycle, driving frantically inside a ball with fire and explosives inside. That is how you will conduct business on a daily basis, learning to work with others flawlessly at high speeds and maneuver with grace as obstacles you never could have foreseen get thrown on your path. And there's no time to train for it. You enter that metal ball on a bicycle with training wheels, thinking, "I've got this." The next thing you know, the lights go down and your bicycle vrooms to life and you are hurtling toward a ring of fire. You'd better gain more speed because getting off is no longer an option. It's a race to the finish.

In the other ring you are surrounded by lions, tigers, and bears. This is no petting zoo. You're not feeding the llamas and bunnies anymore. You're in high boots and a top hat, carrying a crop and trying to appear confident as you walk from animal to animal. If you show weakness, you'll get trampled. Plainly said, you have to know your stuff, or at least look like you do, because these are your investors, and one false move could turn you into their afternoon snack. When one of them roars out of turn, you have to command them to sit and be patient, declaring your next move before they dictate it to you. You have to stay one step ahead, constantly calculating to stay out of the danger zone.

With the crazy all around you in this three-ring circus, it's critical that you stay focused. You have clowns to the right of you, running around, hitting each other over the head, making a mess, oblivious to the distractions they are creating. You have daredevils to the left of you, performing death-defying acts among the explosions, but you cannot wince, because you've got employees whose livelihoods are at stake. In the middle of the insanity you have to be able to make split-second decisions that could make you or ruin you. You have to maintain total control until your finest hour, when you direct every act until its completion and everyone takes their final bow.

Being an entrepreneur is all that and more. I didn't get a best-practices manual. No one told me it would be like this, and there are moments when I feel completely isolated under the big top. I try to keep it all inside, but there are days of monumental stress when everything falls apart and it feels like the moon, the stars, and the whole universe are against me. The business stuff I can handle, most days. But home life is a different story. Look closely, and you'll see that the worry and stress I carry about my family's well-being is the chink in my armor—my biggest weak spot.

Back in the Closet

I'm like any mom, always carrying a little extra guilt that I can't do more. At least fifty other things could have gone wrong at work, and I will somehow manage to hold it together. But all it takes is one dig from Will, intentional or unintentional, about not being present enough for my kids, like missing one of Bella's science projects at school, to push my buttons and send me over the edge and into my closet.

Yes, ma'ams, that's where I go for some privacy when I finally lose my shit. We have five bedrooms, an office, and a finished basement, but my closet is the only place in our house where I can be left alone to have a good, long, heaving cry. It doesn't happen every day, or even every week. It could be building up for months. A few days before, my level of anxiety rises, I can't eat, and I can't sleep. I know when the storm is coming, and it's the perfect place, because the clothes, shoes, and boxes muffle my howls.

Maybe it dates back to when I was a toddler and my daddy played postman with me in my bedroom closet. I have never felt more loved and safe than in those moments. There is something so comforting about that tiny space. I just walk in, sit on the floor, and wail in the dark for as long as it takes to get my release. It might take fifteen minutes, or it might take two hours until it's all out of me and a kind of peace seeps in, as if God is telling me, *Dry your eyes now, there's work to do.* Then I get back up, step out and into the bathroom, and wash my face, ready to conquer the world again.

There will be moments when it all piles up on you. So go ahead and cry. Cry until you are sick of yourself. It's okay to lose it now and then. If you didn't, you wouldn't be human. As long as I can have that momentary release, I am good to go! The pity party never lasts. That's another lesson my brother Donnie taught me. Oh, did I mention how he used to torment me? He was always bringing me back down to earth. Whenever I came back from school and expressed a thought I considered particularly erudite, he'd say, "Oooooh, is that the new college word?" And we'd both burst out laughing.

The worst was when he teased me about my butt. I've always been a size 4, but I was body conscious from the time I was a little girl and obsessed with the fact that I packed a tiny bit extra in the hips. Nothing like Beyoncé or Kim Kardashian, but this was way before junk in the trunk was such a highly prized asset. Knowing what a sore point it was with me, my brother would start singing at the dinner table, "Brandi's got a big ole butt! Yeah! Brandi's got a big ole butt!" On and on it went until I burst into tears and ran into my bedroom.

"Donnie, stop!" my mother would plead, doing her best to hide the fact that she was amused.

"Leave your sister alone!" Daddy would bark.

But he wouldn't stop. He was relentless. Donnie would stand right outside my door, screaming, "Waaaaaah, waaaaaah!" That boy just refused to let me take myself too seriously. It was his way of telling me I had to get over myself and realize how incredibly blessed I was.

Moms in a Jam

Of course, he was right, and still is. I *am* blessed. This incredible journey has been a gift from God, and whenever I need a reminder of why I am here, and what it is all for, I just think of our customers and the many moms and children whose lives we've touched, like one mother of three who had been diagnosed with fibromyalgia, lupus, and congestive heart failure. She was the sole breadwinner of her family, supporting herself, her kids, her aging mother, and a fourteen-month-old grandchild. She was living in constant pain, her immune system had been severely compromised, and yet she still managed to get up every morning to go to work, with a smile on her face. Despite her physical struggles, she was always there for her family. She was their rock.

We gave her a $500 Christmas gift certificate. She was just one of the hundreds of Lolly Wolly Doodle fans we helped get through the holidays as part of our Moms in a Jam giveaway program. Our Facebook members nominate each other and tell their stories, and our team selects those who seem most in need to get $500 and $100 gift cards so that they can pay for gifts for their children and grandchildren.

There are so many deserving people to choose from, and each story chokes me up. The Lolly team is a blubbering mess by the time we've gone through each year's submissions. Like the young mom of a three-year-old girl battling kidney disease. She was running out of resources as she struggled to pay the medical bills. The treatments to keep their daughter alive were so expensive that the woman and her husband were fighting to keep their house. The husband had just run out of paid time off from his job to spend time with his little girl while she was undergoing treatment, which included months of antibiotics, resistant bacterial infections, severe allergic reactions, multiple invasive and painful tests, and reconstructive surgery on her bladder. Now her kidney function is severely compromised, and after more excruciating treatments, she faces the prospect of having a kidney transplant.

Throughout this, this particular mom in a jam had been homeschooling her nine-year-old son and caring for her eight-month-old daughter. She took on an extra job to pay the medical bills for her daughter, as well as the surgery she must now undergo herself to treat her lower-back scoliosis and hip misalignment. As if that wasn't enough misfortune, their car broke down, and it's too expensive to repair. Still, they told us, "God is good, and we know He will provide one way or another."

Where do I stop? The tales are gut wrenching, and the list of those truly in need is endless. These women's lives give us a glimpse into what really goes on in America's heartland. Hardworking families from Missouri, Tennessee, Georgia, and Texas live paycheck to paycheck, and are one health crisis away from losing their homes because their insurance deductibles are so high, even in the rare event their plan covers half the treatments their child or loved one needs to survive.

They are women young and old who are working to put themselves through school while raising children, but can't afford day care. They are wives who have been left with nothing by their husbands, who drove out of state with the family's only car. Now they must get up at dawn to take buses and trains to get to work so that they can put food on the table for their little ones. But they don't complain. Their friends and relatives nominate them for help because they are too proud to ask for it themselves. Instead, they make sacrifices, take extra jobs, and pray to God that somehow, someday things will turn around, and everything is going to be okay.

We get to play a part in bringing a little joy into in the lives of these heroic women, and it is our honor to do so. During the holidays we do as many small acts of kindness for these deserving folks as we can. My family was poor, but they did Christmas like we were billionaires, so the thought of children not waking up Christmas morning to gifts under tree, not thinking they've been good all year, tortures me. And everyone in our Lolly Wolly Doodle family feels the same way.

One Big Family

Each time I give, I am blessed many times over. God has shown me that this is true. A few years back, before all this success happened, I was in the drugstore, down to the last money in my wallet, a hundred-dollar bill. That was grocery money, and it had to stretch far enough to feed me, Will, and our four kids. But there was an older man at the pharmacy counter who couldn't afford to pay for his medication. I felt awful, so I quietly slipped that bill to the pharmacist so that the gentleman could get his prescription filled.

When I had the Temple Spa, I used to keep leftover cash from the register in a secret spot inside my glove compartment. I got back to the car, opened the glove compartment to look for a packet of gum, and two hundred-dollar bills fluttered out. I had no idea the money was still in there. **You cannot out-give God.** I've lived by this giving philosophy ever since.

We all do. The giving makes us feels so good, it's almost selfish. Ask Jamie, Amy, Katie, or anyone on factory floor, and they will all tell you that the biggest reason why they stay on at the Doodle is the honor of blessing others. **It's important for everyone to have little reminders of the lives you are affecting, the larger reason why you are doing what you are doing.** We have a wall between the factory and the warehouse that's lined with notes and pictures of all the people whose lives we've impacted, from the villages in Ecuador that receive our clothing donations, to the little boys and girls who are wearing our outfits as they run to greet their daddies and mommies who are coming back from serving their country in Iraq or Afghanistan. We send outfits and T-shirts for the children of workers who make our cotton goods in China and correspond with letters, pictures, and postcards to give each other glimpses into the lives of families who live halfway around the globe.

It turns out we have far more in common with these folks than not. The factory workers in China and the villagers in Ecuador are doing their best to provide for their kids, just like we are. Our Doodlers understand this in a visceral way. So what began as a small-town start-up is now a part of the big wide world, and although most of our workers have never traveled very far, they feel deeply connected to the people whose lives they have touched. Who knew that the Lolly Wolly Doodle family would grow to be so big?

Being able give back in so many ways makes us all equal at the Doodle. It's a purpose we share, and everyone pitches in with ideas about who to help or where to send extra clothes. Even before Moms in a Jam was a formal program, members of my team would hear tell of someone in the factory struggling to buy presents for her kids, and we'd all pile into my car and drive to Toys "R" Us to pick out some toys and make sure she had plenty to put under her tree. One of our seamstresses told me about a women's shelter here in Davidson County where the moms had nothing for themselves or their kids. Most had to flee abusive relationships with the clothes on their backs, so we regularly send them batches of new clothes for mothers and children in all sizes.

The Giving Tree

And the charity begins at home. It's why we started the Christmas Giving Tree. We always had gift card raffles during our factory holiday parties, but now we give people the option to pay it forward, and they always do.

Everyone looks out for each other. A few years back one of my designers, Erica, who was a seamstress at the time, had to make some major sacrifices. Her husband lost his job before Thanksgiving, and they had to decide between paying tuition for their child's special needs school and selling their home (they sold). Jackie, who worked closely with Erica and acted as a kind of mentor to her, whispered in my ear about the situation. When I called Erica into my office, she was so shy and unassuming. She would never think to burden anyone with her problems or ask for help. But I quietly slipped her a cash card to help pay for the holidays. She was a puddle of tears. We both were.

Beyond the holidays, people in the factory who are struggling have received gift cards and out-of-pocket donations from colleagues who care. When Frank Laney, our machine repairman was struck with cancer, my brother Patrick discovered he was too sick and broke from the special chemo costs to make himself nutritious meals. (It's not uncommon that even folks with decent wage jobs and health insurance plans find themselves in this spot under our country's healthcare system, where the price of life-saving medications not covered by a plan forces them to make some hard choices.) Patrick put together boxes of vegetables and meat from his deep freezer to take to him. When he told me what was going on with Frank, I told him to send him into my office. I gave Frank a big hug and several gift cards to his favorite restaurants.

Frank had showed up at our factory years ago and told me that he had a great job in which he'd been happy for many years, but that God had told him to come and apply for the opening at Lolly Wolly Doodle. I hired him on the spot.

Frank was a man of few words, and not exactly the warm and fuzzy type, but I was drawn to him. That gruff demeanor was clearly a defense for his shyness and humility. Soon everyone fell in love with this salt-of-the-earth character, so when he was plagued with cancer we all prayed and rallied for his healing.

Back then we had great insurance coverage, which paid for his experimental treatment, so we joyfully watched him regain his health. Before long he was looking vibrant again. But I took for granted the differences in health insurance and how the smallest changes in policies could boil down to a matter of life and death, so when we were asked to change the employee plan to one that was more favorable to members of our New York team, I had no clue what could happen. The new coverage was more expensive yet inferior. I didn't know it at the time, but Frank's experimental treatment was immediately denied. After the cage match we switched back again, but it was too late.

The next time you bow to someone's wishes, large or small, things aren't always as insignificant as they appear. Standing up for what you believe in counts on so many levels, and I will never forgive myself for caving in so quickly.

Frank recently came out of the ICU and checked into hospice care for his final days. My heart was so heavy I could feel it dragging me down to the ground because I knew I'd let him down. I had the guts and grit to face just about anything, but not Frank in his final days. If I looked him in the eyes to say good-bye I'd be a blubbering mess, and he'd end up comforting me. It wouldn't be fair.

I grieve for this kind, good, solid man. Then I think about his amazing smile. He didn't break into one often, so you knew he meant it. On several occasions God moved me to bless Frank in different ways, and I never hesitated. Each time he'd come to my office, tell me how much he loved me, and say how uncanny it was how I always knew the exact moment he needed a blessing. If you ever asked him how he was doing, Frank would always give you the sunny side and accept his fate, no matter how much pain he had to endure.

"Brandi, you are such a blessing in keeping me going," he told me one day, after he finally had to go on disability but was still mobile enough to stop by and pay us a visit.

In his last days I wrote him often, sending notes with various workers who happened to be visiting Frank at his hospice bedside when their shift was over to say their good-byes. His replies will be forever in my heart. In his last note to me, he said that *I* inspired *him*. Talk about perspective! As the woman who lived most of her life wanting to be recognized, crowned, and adored, ranking her life by firsts and honors, nothing can compete with being this humble North Carolina machine repairman's inspiration.

I didn't deserve the credit. Those precious office visits from Frank were God's way of showing me that when He speaks, it's our job to listen. Frank came on my path to strengthen my relationship with God. Ah-ha!

So this is why I am sitting here, as CEO of Lolly Wolly Doodle, telling you my story. This is why God gave me this gift of a business that has been transforming lives. Why the heck would he choose me? It wasn't my idea to put those smock dresses up on Facebook, it was His. I can't take credit because He has worked through me, guiding me every step of the way. So when I have one of those closet days and I find myself thinking I'd be better off if I had never left the garage, I turn to my faith, which teaches me that God is never going to give me something I can't handle.

I don't know the full extent of what it is yet, but God had some bigger purpose in mind when He reached out to build this business. At the end of the day, if I didn't believe that this all happened for a reason, you could take everything away and it would be meaningless. This isn't just about rec-reating an apparel model or building a billion-dollar business. This isn't about getting on the covers of magazines. This isn't even about me. It's about showing my kids what we are all capable of and letting them see me try. It's about putting wells in Africa, paying for students to go on field trips, and helping 150 employees feed their families.

One of our former workers just lost her child in a drunk driving accident. The grandmother still works for us. Two women on the sewing floor had double mastectomies in the last six months. They all came back to work right away because being with their Lolly Wolly Doodle family gave them a reason to wake up in the morning. It's what gets them through. It's what gets *me* through. For all of those reasons, and more, I will keep hitting that reset button as many times as He asks me to.

Creating meaningful work for our LWD team of people—every one of them with an incredibly moving story of their own—has been one of the greatest gifts in building this company. And that is really what it is all about for us. Keeping God and our families first, and our many blessings in mind, as we provide our customers with beautiful and affordable clothing that makes their families look great and feel proud, always remembering how important, easy, and fun it is to care about each other and lend a helping hand. These are the values that have kept us grounded throughout this journey and motivated for everything that is still to come.

AH-HA'S

- Remember your purpose and keep it real. When you realize that you have done something that directly affects the lives of others and you get so see their smiling faces after the fact, it touches your heart at the deepest level.

- Hang on to this feeling, because it's all too easy to feel overwhelmed. Anyone who starts, builds, and sustains a business and tries to tell you it's all a joyride is peddling BS.

- As your business or career takes off and you find yourself wishing you could clone yourself, you will struggle to come up with an answer to the riddle of work/life balance. And you have to accept that you may never find it. I don't care how much someone tells you to lean in. When you have children to care for, it's just part of the deal.

- There will be moments when it all piles up on you. So go ahead and cry. Cry until you are sick of yourself. It's okay to lose it now and then. If you didn't, you wouldn't be human. As long as I can have that momentary release, I am good to go!

- Stay focused on the larger reason why you are doing what you are doing. At the Doodle, giving back is the purpose we share, the thing that makes us all equal. It's why we all get up and go to work in the morning.

So give yourself and everyone on your team little reminders of the lives you are affecting.

- Whether it is something as simple as caring for your family, inspiring those around you, creating jobs, or selling a product that makes the lives of others just that little bit better, you are making a difference.

Ten

Value the People on Your Path

Our chief want is someone who will inspire us to be what we know we could be.

–RALPH WALDO EMERSON

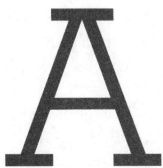t the beginning of this book I talked about ah-ha moments. You know, those events or junctures in life where a switch gets flicked on and it all starts to make sense. They are those points of light on your journey where it everything adds up and you realize things don't happen at random. They are meant to inspire, teach, or put you on a certain path, and the more we pay attention to those large and small signposts from God, the easier it becomes to see the next step to find joy and fulfill our life's purpose.

Well, there are also ah-ha people. Throughout the years I've been blessed to know countless individuals, from my family members and friends to my partners, employees, and customers at the Doodle who've helped light the way for me. They've given me life-altering lessons on humility, compassion, resilience, persistence, and faith—all of those ingredients that make up true scrappiness and grit.

Some were part of key relationships in my life, like my grandmother, Betty, who taught me resourcefulness, generosity, and poise. Or Fran, who showed me how to take a big bite out of life and appreciate every moment. Others I may have only encountered in passing, like small threads woven into the whole fabric. Either way, they made an impression. Although I've already mentioned a few in these last chapters, many of these folks aren't aware of roles they have played on this miraculous journey creating Lolly Wolly Doodle. And there aren't enough pages in this book to talk about every single one. But before I leave you I'd like to share a small sampling—swatches, if you like—to give you a taste of their goodness, humor, and wisdom.

Let's start with our very own Doodler in customer service, Lynn, who in 2010 went face-to-face with a cancer called non-Hodgkin's lymphoma that was hiding between her heart and lungs, and quickly spread to her stomach. First, I must tell you that this is not a depressing story! She had surgery immediately and, after further treatment, has been in remission ever since. It's the grit and determination with which she not only fought the disease but used her experience to help others that moves me and so many others in our Lolly Wolly Doodle community.

Four years before her own diagnosis, Lynn's beloved father had passed away from lung cancer. Then in May 2014 she buried her mom, who died from stomach cancer. Years before, Lynn had made a promise to both of them that she would honor them by participating in Relay for Life, an incredible organization that holds relay races every year to raise funds for cancer research. The problem was, Lynn's mother's funeral was the day before the race. You can imagine how hard it must have been for her to go through with the event after such a painful loss, and she was not planning on doing it again. Yet the Relay for Life event represents so much trial and victory in Lynn's life, from losing her precious parents to winning her own fight again cancer.

Realizing this, my niece Lolly, who works in our social media department, decided to put together a relay team in her honor that Lolly Wolly Doodle would sponsor. She even came up with a name: DoodleLYNN. Now it's an annual tradition for the Doodlers—a way to celebrate Lynn's strength and support the many other cancer survivors and family members in our midst.

Lynn has been involved with Relay for nine years now. Her original team was called Fletcher's Faith, after her Dad. Every year before the race starts, all of the cancer survivors do the honors of taking the first lap, and this is where we stand on the sidelines to cheer Lynn on. We are so grateful she gets to be a part of this group of amazing warriors, and so is Lynn, who thinks about her parents with each and every step. She also thinks about them during the finale of each event, when the organizers light the luminary bags and send them into the night sky with the names of the cancer victims.

"I promised them both that I would 'Relay' for them and I did," she shared with us. "I feel very honored to have LWD sponsor a team for me. I will keep fighting the battle for myself and the ones who are not here with us anymore."

The lesson her actions reinforce for me is that we are all a part of each other's story. Lynn's loss, her battle with cancer, and the courage with which she faced down one of the worst periods of her life moves us all to step up and give back right alongside her. Setting aside her own grief and discomfort, she found a way to help others. It's selfless, uncomplaining Doodlers like Lynn who remind me daily that my own problems are small, and my blessings are infinite. And that we're in this together.

These teachings aren't always quite so profound. Some ah-ha people simply remind us not to take ourselves too seriously. They can break the tension of a bad day and make us laugh at ourselves and the absurdity of life. My big brother Donnie is particularly good at that. Intentionally and unintentionally, he is another member of this cast of inspiring characters, even when he's throwing down one of his outrageous pranks. A few years back he stopped by the factory after one of his forages in a local junkyard (finding treasures in a trash heap is one of this Southern Renaissance man's many interests). Most people were out at lunch that day, but inside one of the offices he found my husband and stepson, Clay, who worked in our social commerce department at the time.

"Hey, Uncle Donnie, what's up?" Clay asked him.

"Got myself a rooster," Donnie told him, delighted to be asked.

Oh, and did I mention that my brother raises chickens on a small parcel of land outside his double-wide? Some of these junkyards have livestock for sale, and Donnie's always looking to add to his collection.

"Ornery fella," Donnie told them. "Won a few cockfights in his day."

Will and Clay looked at each other, smirked, then took the bait.

"Heck, I ain't afraid of no chicken," Clay told him, while Will chuckled.

"Oh yeah? Well, let's see what you got," said Donnie, who dashed back into the parking lot to fetch the rooster from his pickup truck, then chucked the bird inside the office, locking it in with Will and Clay.

For the next few minutes all you could hear were clucks and screams. The rooster won. After they pleaded long enough for mercy, Donnie went inside to take back his prize, leaving behind the devastation of feathers, scattered papers, and two broken egos. The lesson? Don't get cocky! Hah!

My greatest teachers in life have come from the most unexpected places. You'd think my wisest business advice would've come from some expensive, Ivy-League-educated executive coach, but instead I've received these lessons from a humble, down-to-earth local yokel named Steve Summers.

Even though he looked like your average Joe, Steve, a longtime friend of Will's who attends our church, sold his last company—a manufacturer of paper tubes—for more than enough cash to retire himself and his entire family forever. He had some extra time on his hands and was fascinated by the Doodle, so he asked if he could poke around the factory and observe our operations. This man knew how to run the machinery in any factory, and he'd built incredible teams in the factories he'd sold. He also knew how much pressure I was under and, out of the goodness of his heart, offered to help without charging me a dime.

One weekend Will and I were having dinner with Steve and his wife, Rhonda, when I started complaining about the long hours I'd been working.

"I just wish I had a little more help," I whined. "I'm there till late every night and you could hear crickets on that factory floor."

He told me about the time his dad, who was also a brilliant businessman, caught him kneeling on the floor of the factory at 11 p.m., trying to fix a stalled machine. Red-faced and angry, Steve was the only one in the place, alone and working himself to death. The story sounded familiar.

"Boy, what are you doin' here?" he asked Steve.

"I'm fixing the machine because everyone's gone home," Steve huffed.

"Well, it's your own fault," he told him. "If you'd built the right time, you wouldn't be out here all by your lonesome."

Steve got his point across in his usual tactful way. He was right. I didn't have the right people in place. I was so busy trying to meet production deadlines and put out fires all on my own that I hadn't invested the time to build the right systems or processes, so things snowballed and eventually came back on me. Steve helped me put the right people in the right jobs with a whole new infrastructure that would empower us to succeed. It was another blessing that he was put on my path.

I've already shared how our Doodle moms are the embodiment of scrappy as they stretch to make their meager ends meet, putting family first as they cheerfully soldier on, asking for nothing in return. But there's another mom whose selflessness, strength, and love goes beyond anything I've ever witnessed—Lori Cecil, one of my dearest childhood friends.

A few years ago her ten-year-old daughter, Lauren, was killed in a freak pool accident. A power line had gone down somewhere nearby, and an electric current touched a puddle of water, carrying it all the way to the swimming pool where Lauren and her swim team were practicing. The lifeguards heard a sizzle and blew the whistle for all of the kids to come out of the pool. Most jumped over the side, but Lauren was the only one to grab on to the metal pole to pull herself out. It happened instantly, in front of her parents. I cannot imagine what it must have been like to witness your child being taken from you in this horrific way, so quickly and completely out of your control. This was their one and only child, and they were never able to have more children. I just don't know how I would have been able to go on.

But Lori and her husband can see the beauty in every day, in the way they relate to others, to God, and to each other. It's as if they are living an impeccable life in the name of their beloved daughter, helping others and expressing the compassion and love that poured out of this incredible little girl. They started a foundation, Lauren's Ladder, which donates to schools and special needs education all over the state. Lori is a child psychologist, and her first love is helping children. Every year, in Lauren's memory, Will and I go to Walmart, talk to the cashier, find out who has put the most toys on layaway, and pay for them. It's just one of countless quiet little ways Lori gives back to other children and their families.

I first learned about compassion and caring from my own

mother, Pat Tysinger. Mom has always been a big pile of mush, as sentimental as she is crazy. That's another trait we share! Of course, I didn't fully appreciate how much we had in common while I was growing up. We bickered, and I often back-talked or ignored her, more annoyed than chastened when she screamed at me for failing to dry the dishes or put my toys away. All my dad had to say was, "Brandi Rae!" and I would start crying as if my life was over. I grew up in the South when they still did spankings in school, but my father never had to spank me, because his tone would stop me in my tracks. But not Mom's. We were much too alike.

I only started to appreciate our similarities in my late teens. My parents never drank. It's not that they judged other people for having a few cocktails; it's just that they weren't interested. But as a senior in high school I started going to parties and indulged. Mom was so concerned for my safety that she made sure I called her anytime of the night or early morning if I needed a ride. She promised she wouldn't judge if I was out late and a little inebriated. She accepted that is what seniors in high school do, and with so many DUI accidents on the road, she just wanted to make sure I got home in one piece.

One night a group of my girlfriends decided to get together and party. Someone's older brother bought us wine coolers, so my mother made a deal with us. We could drink as long as we stayed at the house for a grown-girl sleepover. I'm not sure where my father was at the time. He was away on either a work or hunting trip. Well, wouldn't you know it. Mom had a sip of wine cooler, and another, and another. She actually got tipsy with us! To this day my friends call her "Pat Seventeen" because she really let her inner seventeen-year-old come out.

There are so many things about my mother I appreciate now that I am an adult. She's amazingly resourceful, like MacGyver. Whenever something needed to be done, she just rolled up her sleeves and did it, whether that was moving around the living room furniture or putting up shelves. This itty-bitty thing, who never weighed more than a hundred pounds, was the epitome of scrappy.

But my favorite thing about my mother is the very characteristic that exasperated me when I was a little girl—her crazy. I was convinced there was a ghost in our house, and no one believed me. Then weird things started happening that we could all see and hear—objects moving from one side of the house to the other, weird knocking noises—and the rest of the family started to wonder if I was telling the truth, especially Mom. After a period when there were a few too many bumps in the night, we were all feeling a bit spooked. There were two bathrooms in our house that shared a wall, and one morning as I was doing my hair and makeup, getting ready for school, I heard my mother's voice on the other side of the wall say, "Brandi . . . ?"

"Mom . . . ?"

"Brandi?!"

"MOM!!!"

I thought I heard terror in her voice, so I ran out of the bathroom screaming. I met up with Mom on our front porch. It was 7 a.m. and we were both still in our pajamas, crying and hugging each other. When we both finally realized that neither of us actually saw anything and we were just reacting to the tone in each other's voices, we started laughing hysterically. I almost peed my pants! It made me realize that sometimes it's not so much what you say but how you say it that can have such a huge impact on someone's emotions.

It was also one of many incidents in my later teen years when I realized that Mom was exactly the person I would want to have alongside me when something kooky was happening. Crazy loves company! There is no question that Pat Seventeen is Mammaw Betty's daughter.

My mammaw taught me to love, appreciate, and accept the eccentricities of others because, let's face it, we're all a little freaky underneath the surface, some more than others.

She was always immaculate—every inch the Southern lady. She never went anywhere without her hair and makeup done. She wore petticoats and hose under her perfectly tailored skirts, with everything matched from her polished shoes to the scarf she wore around her neck. But she was part Cherokee, and every now and then you felt like you were going to get scalped!

My family still talks about the first and last time Mammaw went to my brothers' baseball game. This was before I was born, when Patrick and Donnie were still in elementary school. When she disagreed with a call the umpire made that went against Donnie, she strode right up to where he was standing on the edge of the baseball diamond and started making a fuss.

"You take that back!" she screamed at him. "He threw a foul ball and you know it!"

"It's all right, Betty, don't worry about it," my mortified dad told her as he patted her arm and attempted to gently guide her away from the field.

Now this was long before the days of road rage and angry soccer dads, when public outbursts were not the norm. But that didn't stop my grandmother, who became so irate she chased that poor umpire with her umbrella until he locked himself in his car. The other parents whispered, snickered, and pointed. Mammaw Betty, Miss Manners who was always so concerned with what "they" would think, was all tore up. As hard as she tried to hold herself to the highest standards of conduct, when it came to her family she couldn't help herself.

She was never allowed at one of Patrick or Donnie's sporting events again. Until the very end, whenever she got a little flustered about something, we'd tease her and say, "Uh-oh, Mammaw! Is it time to get out the umbrella again?"

Mom and Mammaw were big on individuality. If I ever had a passion or a conviction about something, they encouraged me to go with it and not half-ass anything. They wanted me to be proud of the things that made me different. But they also taught me to hold a little back, because it's more interesting if not every detail is known.

"Be yourself, do what you enjoy, but hide your crazy," my mother would always say. "People don't need to see everything underneath that table cloth."

Probably one of the biggest ah-ha people in my life has been my oldest, dearest, and best childhood friend, Ashley, who also happens to be my first cousin. My dad and her mother are brother and sister. We lived next door to each other, shared the backyard, and were in and out of each other's houses all day, every day.

I'm a year older than Ashley, and I developed a lot faster when we were kids, both socially and physically. She was this shy, petite thing who tended to be introverted except when she was around me. Like a little yapping puppy, she was constantly trying to get my attention, and it annoyed the heck out of me. Like most "sisters" we had an intense love-hate relationship while we were growing up. While I was dismissive, Ashley lived to get under my skin. It got to the point where we were fighting so much our parents put a mattress in the middle of the yard so that we could wrestle outside.

Even though she was quiet, there has always been a fierce quality to Ashley. You might even say she was fearless. We've already established that I am a total scaredy-cat, and yet my li'l cuz was obsessed with horror movies. One night she had a sleepover with a few of our friends, and she begged me to come over and watch "Jason" with them. I finally relented, but before the first kill scene I ran away screaming and crying, and did a face-plant into a dirt hole my mother had dug earlier that day (it came to be known as the "Watermelon Hole" when Ashley did the same thing while eating a piece or watermelon). For weeks afterward, if Ashley saw me wandering around outside, she'd open her bedroom window, lean out, and loudly whisper, "Kill, kill, kill . . . kill, kill, kill." I crumbled into tears every time.

The balance in our relationship shifted when I was in fifth grade and we were making Barbie doll clothes in my mother's craft room. It was the first time in our lives my parents had left us alone. It was just to go down the street to the store and back, but apparently a lot can happen in ten minutes. My dad had a collection of knives that were so sharp they could split hairs, and I was using one in lieu of sheers to cut fabric when Ashley said something to annoy me.

"Say that again and I'll slice your hand off!" I told her, gesturing with the knife to make my point.

Of course I didn't mean it. But right at that moment Ashley had moved her hand in the direction of the blade and nearly lost two fingers. Blood was pouring everywhere. Her flesh was cut to the bone. And yet Ashley was surprisingly calm. Maybe she was in shock. But I was screaming in horror.

"Ohmigosh, Ashley, I'm so sorry, I'm so sorry!"

When my parents got home to the carnage, Ashley had the presence of mind to cover for me, telling them she wasn't paying attention and her hand had somehow gotten in the way of the knife. She spared them the backstory of our fight and my pretend threats, and she kept it up in the emergency room, when they were stitching her hand back together–and for the rest of our lives. From that moment on, I made a point of being especially nice to her. It was my first lesson on what true loyalty and friendship means. Ashley knew what was in my heart and that I would never have done such a thing on purpose. Our bond was more important to her than telling on me.

Today she's a teacher and has endless patience. Ashley really blossomed and has become the extrovert. While I prefer to stay in when I'm not at work, she's the one out socializing and encouraging me to get out more. She's the one person I can be 100 percent myself with. There's no agenda with her. As busy as I am, she's often the last person on the list I call, but only because I know she understands what my life is like. And when I need her she's right there, by my side. When they got the news that Fran died, it was Ashley and my mom who jumped on a plane–in Ashley's case for the second time in her life–to be in Florida with me the next morning and take care of every last detail.

Ashley is my ah-ha person for unconditional love. Over the years, I've been especially blessed to have friends and family members like her in my corner. I wouldn't have survived this roller coaster without their sanity, support, and humor. It's like the proverb says: "As iron sharpens iron, so one person sharpens another."

By now you probably know I am a huge fan of Pastor Joel Osteen. He has wisdom on any subject you care to Google, including the importance of surrounding yourself with people who make you a better person. In one of my favorite of his sermons, he talks about how there are God-ordained people who inspire us. We can and should choose to surround ourselves with these individuals, because "you can't hang out with chickens and expect to soar like eagles." But "if you hang around excellent people, excellence will rub off on you."

My excellent people lift me up, make me laugh, and tell me the truth when I need to hear it the most. Some are still in my life, some have moved on, but each one gave me a gift of wisdom, helping me to go further than I ever could have imagined. My heart overflows with love gratitude for these people–the Ashleys, Donnies, Loris, Pats, and Steves of my life. Even if I haven't mentioned you by name, you know who you are. Thank-you, thank-you, thank-you for your wisdom, kindness, selflessness, and support. I couldn't have done it without you.

Lolly-isms

I've always been a big fan of inspirational quotes. Each time I scan through Pinterest, I hit on one that seems to speak to me right in that moment. It's almost as if its message was intended just for me, to give me encouragement and perspective when I need it most. Sometimes I'll even come up with my own one-liners, which I share with my Doodle team on Instagram and Facebook. We call them Lolly-isms. As I look back on all the quotes I've posted over the past few years, I realize they tell their own story. Here are a few of my favorites:

Never sacrifice your class to get even with someone who has none.

"Let them have the gutter. You take the high road."
—Unknown

"Never look back. If Cinderella went to pick up her shoe she would not have become a princess."—Unknown

"God can restore what is broken and change it into something amazing. All you need is faith." —Joel 2:25

"There comes a day when you realize turning the page is the best feeling in the world, because you realize there is so much more to the book than the page you were stuck on."—Zayn Malik

Surround yourself with people who have dreams, desire, and ambition: They'll help you push for and realize your own.

"If you ever find yourself in the wrong story, leave."—Mo Willems

"There will be many chapters in your life. Don't get lost in the one you're in now."—Unknown

Life is full of decisions, and the hardest ones are those that define us.

"Mostly it is loss which teaches us about the worth of things."—Arthur Schopenhauer

"Love your whole story even if it hasn't been the perfect fairy tale."—Melanie Moushigian Koulouris

"If you want light to come into your life, you need to stand where it is shining."—Guy Finley

"You will never reach your destination if you stop and throw stones at every dog that barks."—Winston Churchill

"You can't always control who walks into your life, but you can control which window you throw them out of."—Unknown

"Always know the difference between what you're getting and what you deserve."—Unknown

What feels like the end is often the beginning.

We get a new opportunity to make a fresh start every morning. Make the most of it.

Every morning you have two choices: continue to sleep with your dreams or wake up and chase them.

"I believe in being strong when everything seems to be going wrong. I believe that happy girls are the prettiest girls. I believe that tomorrow is another day, and I believe in miracles."—Audrey Hepburn

"If your dreams do not scare you, they aren't big enough."—Ellen Johnson Sirleaf

"The best thing about the future is that it comes one day at a time."—Abraham Lincoln

"Everyone wants happiness. But you can't make a rainbow without a little rain." —Zion Lee

"Behind every successful woman is ... herself."
—Unknown